What Will Suffice

Contemporary American Poets

on the

Art of Poetry

What Will Suffice

Contemporary American Poets

on the

Art of Poetry

EDITED BY
CHRISTOPHER BUCKLEY
AND
CHRISTOPHER MERRILL

GIBBS·SMITH
→P
PUBLISHER

SALT LAKE CITY

First edition
97 96 95   3 2 1

This is a Peregrine Smith Book, published by Gibbs Smith, Publisher
P.O. Box 667, Layton, UT 84041   (801) 544-9800

Design by Kathleen Timmerman

Cover art: *Dante's Chair* by Nadya Brown

Printed and bound in the United States of America

Library of Congress Cataloging-in-Publication Data
What will suffice : contemporary American poets on the art of poetry / edited by
    Christopher Buckley and Christopher Merrill.
        p. cm.
    ISBN 0-87905-692-4 : $17.95
    1. Poetics—Poetry. 2. American poetry—20th century.
I. Buckley, Christopher, 1948-   . II. Merrill, Christopher.
PS595.P62W48   1995
811'.54080357—dc20   95-14830
                                                            CIP

Czeslaw Milosz

Ars Poetica?

I have always aspired to a more spacious form
that would be free from the claims of poetry or prose
and would let us understand each other without exposing
the author or reader to sublime agonies.

In the very essence of poetry there is something indecent:
a thing is brought forth which we didn't know we had in us,
so we blink our eyes, as if a tiger had sprung out
and stood in the light, lashing his tail.

That's why poetry is rightly said to be dictated by a daimonion,
though it's an exaggeration to maintain that he must be an angel.
It's hard to guess where that pride of poets comes from,
when so often they're put to shame by the disclosure of their frailty.

What reasonable man would like to be a city of demons,
who behave as if they were at home, speak in many tongues,
and who, not satisfied with stealing his lips or hand,
work at changing his destiny for their convenience?

It's true that what is morbid is highly valued today,
and so you may think that I am only joking
or that I've devised just one more means
of praising Art with the help of irony.

There was a time when only wise books were read,
helping us to bear our pain and misery.
This, after all, is not quite the same
as leafing through a thousand works fresh from psychiatric clinics.

And yet the world is different from what it seems to be
and we are other than how we see ourselves in our ravings.
People therefore preserve silent integrity,
thus earning the respect of their relatives and neighbors.

The purpose of poetry is to remind us
how difficult it is to remain just one person,
for our house is open, there are no keys in the doors,
and invisible guests come in and out at will.

What I'm saying here is not, I agree, poetry,
as poems should be written rarely and reluctantly,
under unbearable duress and only with the hope
that good spirits, not evil ones, choose us for their instrument.

—translated by Czeslaw Milosz and Lillian Vallee

Table of Contents

Introduction XI

AGHA SHAHID ALI "Ghazal" 1

TOM ANDREWS "Ars Poetica" 2

JOHN ASHBERY "What Is Poetry?" 3

ROBIN BECKER "Dreaming at the Rexall Drug" 4

MARVIN BELL "The Book of the Dead Man (#10)" 6

MOLLY BENDALL "The Hairdresser" 8

ROBERT BLY "The Gaiety of Form" 9

MICHELLE BOISSEAU "Against the Muse" 11

EARL S. BRAGGS "See Spot Run" 13

CHRISTOPHER BUCKLEY "Ars Poetica" 14

RALPH BURNS "The Big Money" 16

HAYDEN CARRUTH "The Impossible Indispensability of
  the Ars Poetica" 17

LUCILLE CLIFTON "here yet be dragons" 18

JUDITH ORTIZ COFER "Letter from My Mother in Spanish" 19

MARK COX "The River" 21

MARY CROW "Westering" 23

ROBERT DANA "In the Gardens of Fabulous Desire" 24

KATE DANIELS "*Ars Poetica*" 28

GLOVER DAVIS "The Fish Tank" 30

FRED DINGS "Redwing Blackbirds" 31

RITA DOVE "Ars Poetica" 32

NORMAN DUBIE "Of Politics, & Art " 33

PETER EVERWINE "How It Is" 34

CAROL FROST "Music for Death" 35

JAMES GALVIN "Art Class" 36

BREWSTER GHISELIN "Credo" 37

JORIE GRAHAM "Subjectivity" 38

LINDA GREGG "The Life of Literature" 43

DONALD HALL "Ox Cart Man" 44

JUDITH HALL "Descendent" 45

SAM HAMILL "Arse Poetica" 46

C.G. HANZLICEK "Osprey" 47

ROBERT HASS "Spring Drawing 2" 50

JUAN FILIPE HERRERA
   "El Secreto de mis Brazos" / "The Secret of My Arms" 52

EMILY HIESTAND "Chain of Species" 53

BRENDA HILLMAN "Little Furnace" 54

EDWARD HIRSCH "Sortes Virgilianae" 55

JANE HIRSHFIELD "Justice without Passion" 56

GARRETT HONGO "Stay with Me" 57

RICHARD HUGO "The House on 15th S.W." 59

LYNDA HULL "Cubism, Barcelona" 61

T.R. HUMMER "Ohio Abstract: Hart Crane" 64

MARK IRWIN "On Language" 67

RICHARD JACKSON "For a Long Time I Have Wanted to
   Write a Happy Poem" 68

JEAN JANZEN "Potato Planting" 71

MARK JARMAN "What Only Poetry Can Do" 72

JUDY JENSEN "Faith" 73

RODNEY JONES "The Bridge" 75

CLAUDIA KEELAN "Ars Poetica" 77

YUSEF KOMUNYAKAA "Safe Subjects" 78

MAXINE KUMIN *Ars Poetica*: A Found Poem" 80

ANN LAUTERBACH "Poem" 81

SYDNEY LEA "Accident" 82

CAROL LEM "Ars Poetica" 84

PHILIP LEVINE "The Simple Truth" 86

LARRY LEVIS "The Poem You Asked For" 87

VICTOR MARTINEZ "Poesia" 88

WILLIAM MATTHEWS "Sad Stories Told in Bars:
   The 'Reader's Digest' Version" 90

COLLEEN J. McELROY "Tapestries" 92

THOMAS McGRATH "Ars Poetica: Or: Who Lives
   in the Ivory Tower?" 95

HEATHER McHUGH "What He Thought" 97

LYNNE McMAHON "Toward Eve" 99

SANDRA McPHERSON "Two Men Trading Dance Movements
   at Tabby's Blues Box and Heritage Hall, Baton Rouge" 101

W.S. MERWIN "Air" 104

CAROL MUSKE "To the Muse" 105

CHAD ONESS "Pulling in the Nets" 108

WALTER PAVLICH "Stan Laurel Tutors a Would-Be Comedian" 110

LUCIA MARIA PERILLO "The Roots of Pessimism in Model Rocketry,
   The Fallacy of Its Premise" 112

DONALD REVELL "Consenting" 114

ALBERTO RÍOS "Teodoro Luna's Two Kisses" 115

DAVID RIVARD "And Continuing" 117

LEN ROBERTS "Shoveling while the Snow Keeps Falling" 119

MARGARITA LUNA ROBLES "And Language Can't Find Me" 121

PATTIANN ROGERS "Reaching the Audience" 122

MARIÈVE RUGO "On Not Being Able to Write" 124

MURIEL RUKEYSER "To Enter that Rhythm Where the
    Self is Lost" 125

DIXIE SALAZAR "For a Blow Up Doll Found in a Canal" 127

DENNIS SALEH "The Unconscious" 129

LUIS OMAR SALINAS "Sometimes Mysteriously" 130

SHEROD SANTOS "Abandoned Railway Station" 131

DENNIS SCHMITZ "Because the Eye is a Flower Whose Root
    is the Hand" 132

PETER SEARS "Lip's Lounge" 133

EVE SHELNUTT "Nature, One Might Say" 134

NAOMI SHIHAB NYE "Problems with the Story" 136

CHARLES SIMIC "Prodigy" 137

MAURYA SIMON "Ars Poetica" 138

GARY SOTO "Braly Street" 139

ROBERTA SPEAR "Diving for Atlantis" 142

ELIZABETH SPIRES "The Woman on the Dump" 144

WILLIAM STAFFORD "The Old Writers' Welcome to the New" 146

GERALD STERN "Another Insane Devotion" 147

DAVID ST. JOHN "Gin" 149

CHASE TWICHELL "Word Silence" 151

JON VEINBERG "Stickball Till Dawn" 153

ANN VNUCAK "Ars Poetica" 155

ELLEN BRYANT VOIGT "Song and Story" 157

DIANE WAKOSKI "With Words" 159

BRUCE WEIGL "The Impossible" 162

DAVID WOJAHN "Human Form" 164

CHARLES WRIGHT "Ars Poetica" 166

JAMES WRIGHT "Ars Poetica: Some Recent Criticism" 166

ROBERT WRIGLEY "Poetry" 173

GARY YOUNG "Seven Days: An Ars Poetica" 175

Acknowledgments and Copyright Notices 177

Introduction

IT WAS WALLACE STEVENS WHO ASSERTED THAT "POETRY IS THE SUBJECT OF THE POEM"—the point of departure for this gathering of poems and reflections on the art of poetry. Indeed, the whole of Stevens's work—*The Whole of Harmonium*, as he wanted to call his *Collected Poems*—is devoted to that subject and thus amounts to a grand ars poetica, each part of which illustrates or explains how "The poem refreshes life." The man who spent his days working as an insurance executive in Hartford, Connecticut and nights meditating on poetry's place in the modern age was perhaps our greatest celebrant of the literary genre most firmly ensconced on the margins of our culture. *What Will Suffice* is a testament to his enduring vision.

Central to Stevens's project was his belief that poetry can play a significant role in our changing relations to the world. The rise of science and technology; the decline of traditional religious practice—"The death of one god is the death of all," he declared; the acceleration of history and horror—these continue to torment men and women, and Stevens thought that poetry might counter the despair born of that sense of meaninglessness. "From this the poem springs," he wrote: "that we live in a place/ That is not our own and, much more, not ourselves/ And hard it is in spite of blazoned days."

Estranged from our surroundings and from ourselves, we must turn to poetry, according to Stevens, to forge new connections between the imagined and the real, uniting disparate elements of our experience through sound and rhythm, image and metaphor. Here is how he begins "Of Modern Poetry," his most direct statement about his art:

> The poem of the mind in the act of finding
> What will suffice. It has not always had
> To find: the scene was set; it repeated what
> Was in the script.
> Then the theatre was changed
> To something else. Its past was a souvenir.

Poetry, in this view, depends on discovering, moment by moment, ways of being: improvisation, not recitation. The same holds for our approach to life itself.

It was not always like this, or so he imagined. Surely one of his "souvenirs" was Horace's *Ars Poetica*, which after twenty centuries still haunts and inspires those who write about the art of poetry. Its 476 lines are by turns lyrical and savage, meditative and acerbic; it is at once a labyrinth of ideas and a musical thread readers follow to escape Time's various forms of the Minotaur. This poem is the fountainhead for the vital tradition of poets declaring their aims and independence; composed in the face of Rome's relinquishment of freedom, it is an eloquent defense of civil liberties. Its contradictions and satiric jabs are its emblems of order and energy. "Writers!" Horace commands in Burton Raffel's witty translation. "Write what you can, and/ Think: can you really? really?" Elsewhere he explains that,

> In time, our poets tried everything, dared
> To be different from Homer,
> Sang Latin, sang Roman,
> Some of them sang cheerful, some sang sad,

> Many, many sang well. And Rome would rule
> The world of letters, too, if our poets—
> All our poets, friends: all—could stop
> To blot and erase. My friends:
>> Lock your desk
> On uncorrected lines; poems written nine times over
> Are nothing, ten is only the beginning.

Rome, of course, fell, and in retrospect it is possible to imagine these lines containing not only a moral imperative but also a political obligation. Writing well, with as much courage, depth, honesty, passion, and musicality as they can muster, is how poets contribute to the health—cultural, spiritual, political—of a society. "Let me play grindstone instead of cutting edge," Horace suggests. "At least a grindstone sharpens steel." His *Ars Poetica* is, indeed, a grindstone against which we may yet sharpen our wits.

Certainly it left its share of sparks in the work of Alexander Pope, whose "Essay on Criticism" is the Enlightenment's exemplary ars poetica. Written in heroic couplets, it is in fact an essay on poetics as well as on what the poet envisions as the "Rules for the Conduct of Manners in a Critic"—namely, candor, modesty, good breeding, sincerity, and freedom of advice. "True Ease in Writing comes from Art, not Chance," Pope claims, "As those move easiest who have learn'd to dance." Thus he makes plain the steps a poet must learn before attempting to dance in verse:

> *True Wit* is *Nature* to Advantage drest,
> What oft was *Thought*, but ne'er so well *Exprest*,
> *Something*, whose Truth convinc'd at Sight we find,
> That gives us back the Image of our Mind,

and:

> *Words* are like *Leaves*; and where they most abound,
> Much *Fruit* of *Sense* beneath is rarely found.

and:

> In *Words*, as *Fashions*, the same Rule will hold;
> Alike Fantastick, if *too New*, or *Old*;
> Be not the *first* by whom the *New* are try'd,
> Nor yet the *last* to lay the *Old* aside.

But it is Pope's advice about prosody—the art of versification—that most interests many poets. Convinced that "The *Sound* must seem an *Eccho* to the *Sense*," he describes, and enacts, how tone-deaf writers mangle their lines:

> These *Equal Syllables* alone require,
> Tho' oft the Ear the *open Vowels* tire,
> While *Expletives* their feeble Aid *do* join,
> And ten low Words oft creep in one dull Line,
> While they ring round the same *unvary'd Chimes*,
> With sure *Returns* of still *expected Rhymes*.
> Where-e'er you find *the cooling Western Breeze*,
> In the next Line, it *whispers thro' the Trees*;
> If *Chrystal Streams with pleasing Murmurs creep*,
> The Reader's threaten'd (not in vain) with *Sleep*.

Then, at the *last*, and *only* Couplet fraught
With some *unmeaning* Thing they call a *Thought*,
A *needless Alexandrine* ends the Song,
That like a wounded Snake, drags its slow length along.

The joke, of course, is that Pope slips an alexandrine into that last slow line, and then he demonstrates how in the best work sound echoes sense:

Soft is the Strain when *Zephyr* gently blows,
And the *smooth Stream* in *smoother Numbers* flows;
But when loud Surges lash the sounding Shore,
The *hoarse, rough Verse* shou'd like the *Torrent* roar.
When *Ajax* strives, some Rock's vast Weight to throw,
The Line too *labours*, and the Words move *slow*;
Not so, when swift *Camilla* scours the Plain,
Flies o'er th'unbending Corn, and skims along the Main.

The seeming ease with which the poet captures the physical presence of a subject—slowing or quickening his verses with the judicious use of stressed and unstressed syllables, then imitating, through his arrangement of vowels and consonants, sounds associated with, say, a crashing wave—is nothing short of dazzling. In the last line, for example, Pope again resorts to an alexandrine to make a point, though now his verse sails by with so much speed that careless readers may not notice its extra foot. Such expressiveness within strict formal limits is a hallmark of the Augustan style, which was based—at least in theory—on (among other things) a classical reading of the ancients, Horace included, and "An Essay on Criticism" is a primer on its particular graces. Like any ars poetica, it seeks to educate its readers, tuning their ears to the poetic subtleties—imaginative and prosodic—of the age. Like all masterpieces, it transcends its time, arguing in the most discriminating fashion—and with the lightest possible touch—for a standard of literary excellence best exemplified by its own lines.

Pope's cautionary tale is balanced in the Romantic era by William Wordsworth's *Prelude*, a book-length treatise on the growth of the poet's mind. If Pope was concerned with manners, social and poetic, Wordsworth was consumed—in roughly equal measures—with nature and the French Revolution. "Fair seedtime had my soul," he confesses, "and I grew up/ Fostered alike by beauty and by fear"—by nature, that is, which, like revolution, is Janus-faced, offering on the one hand solace and intellectual sustenance and, on the other, sheer terror. *The Prelude*, which was originally planned to be the autobiographical introduction to an unfinished long philosophical poem entitled *The Recluse*, relentlessly examines the ways in which the poet was shaped by his experiences in the wilds of nature, in London, and in the French Revolution. While this poem belongs to the tradition of the spiritual autobiography, it is also Wordsworth's ars poetica, wherein he shows how "The mind of man is fashioned and built up/ Even as a strain of music." Nor was he afraid to affirm his faith in nature's conflicting powers:

I believe
That there are spirits which, when they would form
A favored being, from his very dawn
Of infancy do open out the clouds
As at the touch of lightning, seeking him
With gentle visitation—quiet powers,

Retired, and seldom recognized, yet kind,
And to the very meanest not unknown—
With me, though, rarely in my boyish days
They communed. Others too there are, who use,
Yet haply aiming at the self-same end,
Severer interventions, ministry
More palpable—and of their school was I.

"Severer interventions"? In Wordsworth's childhood they assumed the form of haunting encounters with nature, which left him "with a dim and undetermined sense/ Of unknown modes of being." In later life those ministrations came in the wake of his adventures in the city and under the Reign of Terror, which shattered his poetic faculties. *The Prelude* charts that crisis of imagination and taste, relating how poetry's sources can be "Impaired and Restored." The climax is unlike any other in English poetry prior to that time:

There are in our existence spots of time,
That with distinct pre-eminence retain
A renovating virtue, whence—depressed
By false opinion and contentious thought,
Or aught of heavier or more deadly weight,
In trivial occupations, and the round
Of ordinary intercourse—our minds
Are nourished and invisibly repaired;
A virtue, by which pleasure is enhanced,
That penetrates, enables us to mount,
When high, more high, and lifts us up when fallen.
This efficacious spirit chiefly lurks
Among those passages of life that give
Profoundest knowledge to what point, and how,
The mind is lord and master—outward sense
The obedient servant of her will. Such moments
Are scattered everywhere, taking their date
From our first childhood.

Nobel laureate Octavio Paz reminds us that "the public religion of modernity has been Revolution, while its private religion has been poetry." Wordsworth was among the first to recognize and describe the consequences of this historic change. His was a poetry rooted in nature, yet he could not avoid the trappings and allure of revolution, which drew him away from his beloved Lake District and nearly ruined his poetic gift. Fortunately, he managed to turn that upheaval into verse, linking public and private matters, forging a new religion of poetry—a tradition that has no shortage of believers in America. For ours is a country founded on religious and revolutionary principles alike, while remaining dedicated to the preservation of individual liberties and rights: fertile ground for the rise and cultivation of any number of spiritual impulses, including poetry.

"I celebrate myself," Walt Whitman announces at the beginning of "Song of Myself," our earliest genuine poem *and* ars poetica, "And what I assume you shall assume,/ For every atom belonging to me, as good belongs to you." Who was this representative man? "Walt Whitman, an American, one of the roughs, a kosmos," he reveals in the twenty-fourth section, which also contains some of his most explicit writing on the art of poetry:

> I speak the pass-word primeval. . . . I give the sign of democracy;
> By God! I will accept nothing which all cannot have their counterpart
>   of on the same terms.
>
> Through me many long dumb voices,
> Voices of the interminable generations of slaves,
> Voices of prostitutes and of deformed persons,
> Voices of the diseased and despairing, and of thieves and dwarves,
> Voices of cycles of preparation and accretion,
> And of the threads that connect the stars—and of wombs, and of the
>   fatherstuff,
> And of the rights of them the others are down upon,
> Of the trivial and flat and foolish and despised,
> Of fog in the air and beetles rolling balls of dung.
>
> Through me forbidden voices,
> Voices of sexes and lusts. . . . voices veiled, and I remove the veil,
> Voices indecent by me clarified and transfigured.

Whitman's poet, speaking in the rhythms of the King James Bible, is a vessel for all of the voices of democracy, especially for those that do not receive a proper hearing in the public dialogue essential to the maintenance of freedom and the perpetuation of democratic ideals. One such voice belonged to his poetic counterpart, Emily Dickinson, who did not need his bardic yawp to speak memorably about the human condition; although her work remained unpublished until long after her death, it has taken its rightful place in the unfolding life of our culture, and her influence on succeeding generations of poets has been as decisive as that of the so-called father of American poetry. "The proof of a poet is that his country absorbs him as affectionately as he has absorbed it," Whitman wrote in his preface to the first edition of *Leaves of Grass*. Dickinson's proof is as elegant as Whitman's is forceful: our literature and our future depend on both. Her most famous version of an ars poetica is a staple of the poetry workshop:

> Tell all the Truth but tell it slant—
> Success in Circuit lies
> Too bright for our infirm Delight
> The Truth's superb surprise
> As Lightning to the Children eased
> With explanation kind
> The Truth must dazzle gradually
> Or every man be blind—

The "dazzling" truths of our time make it difficult for anyone to see, and Dickinson's advice to poets, inscribed in the same hymn-book measures she knew from her Congregational church, is useful for all who do not want to avert their eyes from the shifting perspectives offered by modernity. Scores of poets have since focused on "Truth's superb surprise," which over the last hundred years has not always or even often been superb. But it has been astonishing, which may help explain why the element of surprise has become so important to poets in the twentieth century. The French Surrealists fashioned an entire poetics out of the unexpected, and it is common for writers everywhere to describe their work in terms of the discoveries they make. "The room of marvels," André Breton's apt definition of poetry, is at least as large as the earth itself.

How to explain the sheer number of modern poets investigating their own means of expression? Whenever historic changes are afoot, poets are usually near the forefront of those determined to understand the nature of those changes. Ours is an age in which everything—politics and religion, culture and morality, space and time—is questioned; it is only natural for poets to occasionally question that which is in itself a quest of the most ephemeral kind. W. S. Merwin wrote of poetry that "No one can has any claims on it, no one deserves it, no one knows where it goes." That uncertainty is at the heart of the poetic enterprise, and any answers poets furnish regarding their art, provisional though they may be, become maps for readers, guides to the unknown.

While Archibald MacLeish was certain that "A poem should not mean/ But be," Marianne Moore professed to "dislike" the whole genre: "there are things that are important beyond all this fiddle," she sighed. "Reading it, however, with a perfect contempt for it, one discovers in/ it after all, a place for the genuine." And her poetry, needless to say, is a river teeming with the genuine. "I think it is high time that everybody/ With a true love of rime assert his views," Karl Shapiro decided "In the midcentury of our art," and so he composed a book-length *Essay on Rime*. What did he believe? "Each writer is . . . / An arbiter of the tongue; not a free hand,/ Not an authority, but, by grace of ear,/ One who lends emphasis to forms." Meanwhile, Czeslaw Milosz added a question mark to his "*Ars Poetica?*" to accentuate the conditional nature of his project. All the same, the Nobel laureate has firm ideas about his art:

> The purpose of poetry is to remind us
> how difficult it is to remain just one person,
> for our house is open, there are no keys in the doors,
> and invisible guests come in and out at will.

And Kenneth Koch's "The Art of Poetry," a veritable feast of ideas and impressions that is unfortunately too long to include in this anthology, recommends that "A reader should put your work down puzzled/ Distressed, and illuminated, ready to believe/ It is curious to be alive."

A poem is a moral and mythic construct. Each decision the writer makes concerning subject matter, form, diction, and tone reveals something about his or her vision of the world. Nowhere is that vision more on display than in an ars poetica, which is where a poet takes stock, writing down his or her articles of faith. An ars poetica is also a barometer for the cultural climate of one's times, and what the "readings" contained in this book suggest about post-Cold War America is that there are countless ways to interpret and transform our experiences. In the new world order the theater has changed yet again: the rise of ethnic conflict, neofascism, nationalism, and religious fundamentalism; the depletion of the earth's resources and devastation of innumerable ecosystems; continuing economic problems in both the developed and developing parts of the world; overpopulation; the spread of AIDS and other communicable diseases;—these are dangers everyone faces. And poets are finding, in small ways and large, what will suffice for the next act.

Christopher Merrill

Agha Shahid Ali

Ghazal

The only language of loss left in the world is Arabic—
These words were said to me in a language not Arabic.

Ancestors, you've left me a plot in the family graveyard—
Why must I look, in your eyes, for prayers in Arabic?

Majnoon, his clothes ripped, still weeps for Laila.
Oh, this is the madness of the desert, his crazy Arabic.

Who listens to Ishmael? Even now he cries out:
Abraham, throw away your knives, recite a psalm in Arabic.

From exile Mahmoud Darwish writes to the world:
You'll all pass between the fleeting words of Arabic.

The sky is stunned, it's become a ceiling of stone.
I tell you it must weep. So kneel, pray for rain in Arabic.

At an exhibition of Mughal miniatures, such delicate calligraphy:
Kashmiri paisleys tied into the golden hair of Arabic!

The Koran prophesied a fire of men and stones.
Well, it's all now come true, as it was said in the Arabic.

When Lorca died, they left the balconies open and saw:
his qasidas braided, on the horizon, into knots of Arabic.

Memory is no longer confused, it has a homeland—
Says Shammas: Territorialize each confusion in a graceful Arabic.

Where there were homes in Deir Yassein, you'll see dense forests—
That village was razed. There's no sign of Arabic.

I too, Oh Amichai, saw the dresses of beautiful women.
And everything else, just like you, in Death, Hebrew, and Arabic.

They ask me to tell them what "Shahid" means—
Listen: it means "The Belovéd" in Persian, "Witness" in Arabic.

The Belovéd Witness

BECAUSE I'VE BEEN THROWN INTO THE POST-COLONIAL WORLD, WHICH IS SIMPLY NOT post-enough, I invent a homeland, my homelands, constantly, on both sides of the ocean (but are there only two sides?). This, the expatriate's condition, is often intoxicating. Drunk with forms, images, and rhythms—both those left behind and those that greet one (at times like office functionaries but often, caressingly, like lovers)—one plays the incidental role of witness. How to turn that part into a consummate moment so that one

1

is cosmopolitan but not affected, so that one is personal-emotional-cultural-political but neither rhetorical nor artificial? My work aspires thus. I offer "Ghazal." In my ghazal (which is true, though not entirely, to the form), the *makhta*, at the end, offers my—dare I call it?—poetics. The accidents of history, many of them deliberate, have put me in the enviable—isn't it? is it?—situation of contributing simultaneously to three rising traditions: the new Anglophone literatures of the world, the new subcontinental literatures in English, and the new multi-ethnic literatures of the United States. So I tell the truth, not always all of it, slant. I play my role of witness. But I never lose sight of the sensuousness—the ecstatic tradition of the Sufis'—that *belovéd* confers on me. No minimalism for me, then. And my poetics? Lover and belovéd at once, witness of three worlds, each, from the beginning, mine: Hindu, Islamic, and Western. These I distill in exile.

⌁❦⌁

Tom Andrews

Ars Poetica

The dead drag a grappling hook for the living.
The hook is enormous. Suddenly it is tiny.
Suddenly one's voice is a small body falling
through silt and weeds, reaching wildly. . .

JAMES THURBER WAS ONCE INTERVIEWED BY A REPORTER WHO HAD READ THURBER IN A French translation; after reading Thurber in English, the reporter said he preferred the French translation. "That's always been my problem," Thurber replied. "I lose something in the original." While writing a poem, I hope to be confronted with a moment when, as William Stafford put it, "the material talks back," often frustrating my original intent or design for the poem. At that moment I have a decision to make. I can insist on my original intent or I can try to listen to and follow the poem's emerging direction. Invariably I find that if I insist on my original design, then "I lose something in the original." Increasingly I'm interested in letting my poems (as in "Ars Poetica") engage directly this tension between my own desire to speak and the language's tendency to displace the speaker. The more I write, the more I discover the truth of something Michel Focault wrote: "Language always seems to be inhabited by the other, the elsewhere, the distant."

⌁❦⌁

2

John Ashbery

What Is Poetry?

The medieval town, with frieze
Of boy scouts from Nagoya? The snow

That came when we wanted it to snow?
Beautiful images? Trying to avoid

Ideas, as in this poem? But we
Go back to them as to a wife, leaving

The mistress we desire? Now they
Will have to believe it

As we believe it. In school
All the thought got combed out:

What was left was like a field.
Shut your eyes, and you can feel it for miles around.

Now open them on a thin vertical path.
It might give us—what?—some flowers soon?

Robin Becker

Dreaming at the Rexall Drug

In Wyoming, at the confluence
of Clear and Piney Creeks, I find myself
watching low clouds mass above the Bighorns.
If I were to get on the bicycle
and ride to Buffalo

I'd saunter into the Rexall Drug
and order a root beer float, I'd fill out
a contest form to win a thoroughbred
as I did every week in my eighth year,
in love with the bay in the plate glass window.

In Buffalo, Wyoming, an America
my Russian grandmother never imagined,
we are standing before the cosmetics
counter, and she is testing Revlon
lipsticks to find the perfect shade of peach.

I drift towards the comic books where Lois Lane
is repeatedly rescued and flies—
as I have started to fly in my dreams—
past skyscrapers and suspension bridges.
My grandmother takes my hand and we walk.

At the house, it's nineteen fifty-five and
my father has the thick black hair he lost
before I was born. He leads us to the
patio where Chinese lanterns sway
like soft paper crowns. All the neighbors I

will grow to love are laughing and floating
in the buoyant atmosphere, and here comes
my mother in a party dress, holding
my baby sister. I've not learned to read
their faces for bankruptcy or grief.

As far as I know, everyone will live
forever, and little girls like me
will continue to win racehorses
from Rexall, where my grandmother will stand,
twisting lipstick tubes, discovering one

imperfect color after another.

IN THIS POEM, THE SPEAKER TRAVELS BACKWARDS IN TIME TO EXAMINE HER PAST AND RECAST IT in light of present knowledge. There she finds familiar characters and settings, the plate glass of her hometown drug store and the colorful lipsticks. Imagination allows the speaker to meet her Russian grandmother in Wyoming, and her bald father is suddenly refurbished with a full head of thick hair. These magical transformations are juxtaposed alongside the facts she does not change: as a child, she was ignorant of grief; she had no understanding of death and believed that people lived forever. Beneath the memorable details of Chinese lanterns, familiar neighbors, and the mother's party dress is an undercurrent of sadness. Bankruptcy and grief, mortality and loss undercut the rich details. The poem closes with an image of frustration and dissatisfaction in which the beloved grandmother searches in vain for the "perfect" object, the unattainable ideal.

The speaker's journey parallels the poet's journey. The Rexall Drug Store in Wyoming is the catalytic setting for the speaker's meditation and suggests the way a place, an image, or a word may trigger a poem. The poet must "re-invent" experience, relying on vivid detail and the senses. Like the speaker in the poem, the poet works alone and creates—out of solitude—a habitable world. Frequently, for me, poetry involves confronting the sorrowful and melancholy aspects of family life, using retrospection to illuminate and texture an otherwise flat picture. In poems, time may contract or expand; forgotten memories may rise up to form iconic images. The art of poetry allows us to fly as well as walk, to be old and young at once, to be inside and outside personal experience. And in poetry we may combine the real and the ideal, the concrete and the abstract. As the title of this poem suggests, poetry invites us to "dream" our way into the rich material of our lives.

The Book of the Dead Man (#10)

1. *About the Dead Man and His Poetry*

The dead man has poetry in his stomach, bowels and genitals.
In the dead man's inner organs, poems are born, mate, change and die.
The dead man's genitalia have caused him many problems.
When the dead man's writing is called "poetry," he laughs derisively.
The dead man sees no difference between a line and a sentence.
The dead man distributes definitions of poetry by reshaping the concept.
"Oh Dead Man, Dead Man," sings the nightingale of tradition.
"Dead Man, oh Dead Man," sing the masses of sparrows.
The dead man, like Keats, shall live among the English poets.
The dead man is perfected fallibility, the dead man shines without reflecting,
      the dead man is one of one, two of two, three of three, etc.

2. *More About the Dead Man and His Poetry*

When the dead man writes a poem worth preserving, he immediately burns it.
The dead man burns everything he writes, but pieces survive.
The fragment is more than the whole.
It takes its place among the apocrypha.
The dead man's poems are studied as if he were Aristotle and their subject
      catharsis.
For every book, there is one poem that sells it: a love poem or a life poem.
The dead man writes a poem to woo them in.
The dead man doesn't need to do life-writing. Oh windswept plains!
In the dead man's lexicon, a simple word for a thing, such as "tree," goes
      everywhere: its roots into history and pre-history, its branches into
      entropy and time, its leaves into beauty and belief.
The dead man looks into a cup of coffee and sees the plains of Africa, and of
      course his face appears too.
When he looks down, there appear to him, in the panel of such substance as
      his vision encloses, the matter and the matter-with, events and their
      nature, the beginnings of inertia and the end of momentum.
The entire world starts from the dead man's fingertips and from the front edges
      of his toes, and in all things possible there is a foreground right in front
      of his eyes.
The dead man refutes those who say they have nothing to say, no subject, no
      data, no right, no voice except they first dip their feet in the Ganges or
      tramp the Yukon.
The dead man sees the world in a grain of sand and feels it pass through his
      hands.
He is the unblinking mystic of fiber, fluid and gas.
No manifestation bypasses his bottomless hourglass.

Preface to *The Book of the Dead Man*

"Live as if you were already dead."

BEFORE THE DEAD MAN, MINUS-1 WAS STILL AN IMAGINARY NUMBER.

The Dead Man will have nothing more to do with the conventional Ars Poetica, that blind manifesto allegiant to the past. Let the disenchanted loyalist reconsider the process. Among motives, occasions, codes, needs and knuckle-head accidents, the Dead Man accepts all and everything. He knows in his bones that writing is metabolic.

What are we to make of the Dead Man's reference to Keats? That poetry should come, as Keats wrote, "as naturally as the Leaves to a tree"? To this the Dead Man has added the dimension of the minus. He understands that fallibility and ignorance are the true stores, the bottomless reservoirs of creation. He is the fount *for* that spillover. As for the tedium of objects distorted from their long imprisonment in books, the Dead Man has learned that to be satiated is not to be satisfied.

So he furthers the love affair between the sentence and the line. Whereas formerly the line took a missionary position, under the rule of the Dead Man the sentence once more invigorates the line. The ongoing attempt by dictionary makers to define "poetry," as it has been called, is an object of derision to the Dead Man. The Dead Man knows that every technique is passé except when reencountered at its birth. The Dead Man moves as comfortably among nightingales as among house wrens.

"Perfected fallibility": that's the key, the solace, the right number (one of one, two of two, three of three, etc.). Hence, the fragment is more than the whole. The Dead Man is a material mystic. His hourglass is bottomless. No. 27 ("About the Dead Man and *The Book of the Dead Man*") reminds us that the Dead Man is "a postscript to closure," and "the resident tautologist in an oval universe that is robin's-egg-blue to future generations."

Has it not already been stated of the Dead Man in the poem "About the Dead Man and His Poetry" that he is the tautologist, the postscript, perfected fallibility, etc.? Yes. The Dead Man tells the truth the first time. The Dead Man, too, writes as he has to—with a watch cap and a sweat shirt, with a leaking skull and dilapidated lungs, at an hour beyond clocks. He lives on hunger. He eats his words.

Before the birth of the Dead Man, it was not possible to return. It was not possible, it was pre-conceptual, it was discretionary to the point of chaos and accident to return, since of course there was nowhere yet to return to. Since the birth of the Dead Man, however, it is possible, even likely, that one may return. From the future, one walks ever more slowly into the past.

All this the Dead Man knows. As for me, I know nothing. But do not think one can know nothing so easily. It has taken me many years.

The Hairdresser

It was harder this time:
she wanted something hieratic and memorial.
I'd then cleave and launch a pedestal,
but first unwrap the fearing wastes.
Calling it up by tunes, hoping
to clip raggedy sleeves into
half-full crescents, I propelled it
using paper-cuts of orange.

She said she preferred the burning
poison elsewhere. I, answering
impromptu: "Only a step
to emerge at a later course
in this cosmetic antidote."
With a harp-sweet at the brow,
I pulled darkly until it sparked,
like an adagio in winter.

Finally, wings lay behind
the ears, shivering like prey
and rasping their singular scent.
At once a balustrade
and lamed mandarin revealed
themselves. My optical deception!
Next, I latched the drift grandly—
a feline jewel—against the brittle
gourmet air, and I let her go, blushing.

FOR ME, THE CREATING OF A POEM IS ABOUT THE CONJURING OF THE UNKNOWN, WHICH involves the discovery of hidden colors and hidden currents. Then there is the decision of what to enhance and what to cover up. The challenge and excitement come in not knowing how the mystery of a poem might yield to certain verbal arrangements or how an incarnation of particular sensibility will emerge.

The taming of a poem, however, is always illusory because language contains so much history, so many paradoxes, and so many memories that it inevitably must remain in flux. Finally, the work, the process, is so engrossing that what is revealed in the end is often a surprise.

The Gaiety of Form

1.

How sweet to weight the line with all these vowels!
Body, Thomas, the codfish's psalm. The gaiety
Of form lies in the labor of its playfulness.
The chosen vowel reappears like the evening star
Daily in the solemn return the astronomers love.
When "ahm" returns three times, then it becomes
A note; then the whole stanza turns to music.
It comforts us, says: "I am here, be calm."

2.

"In the sad heat of noon the pheasant chicks
Spread their new wings in the moon dust."
When we choose so, the vowel has its own husband
And children, its nooks and garden and kitchens.
The smoking table gives plebeian sweets
Never equalled by the chocolates French diners
Eat at evening, and gives us pleasures abundant
As Turkish pears picked in the garden in August.

WE RECOGNIZE GOOD SENSE IN POEMS, AND THEN WE ALSO RECOGNIZE MAGIC. IT'S TRUE THAT there is a way of speaking that "makes the poem work," but that's not what we admire in ancient poetry. We all know and value appropriate diction, metaphors that open doors for us, and original thinking that gives a piquant flavor to poems; but we don't honor Virgil or Milton for that. Sometimes a man's or woman's mind, when well-practiced and relaxed, begins to move spontaneously, and words come out beautifully, each word beautifully joined to the other, which catch, as if in a net or a basket, the fish of our feelings at the moment the poet is writing; what a marvel, and yet that is not what we love in Sappho or Anacreon or *Beowolf.* My guess is that what we love is magic. My own sense of what is lovable in great poetry has changed considerably over the years. There was much good poetry written during the Fifties; what seemed to me missing and what I loved particularly was the image as it comes forward in Lorca or in Georg Trakl. I still love the image, and I value tremendously the depth that it brings to a poem when compared either with abstract language, discursive language, or symbolic language. But more and more I love the magic that comes not from the incredible spontaneity of the soul but from the vibrations and harmonies that come from the structures of sound itself, something quite outside the human soul. We know that there was a room in Persia during the Middle Ages that, when a person walked into it, he or she would break into tears in a few moments. Yet there were no symbols, images, paintings or statues in the room. The emotions were pulled out of the soul by proportions of volume, that is to say by the impersonal relationships between inches, feet and yards. In other words, the composition was impersonal. We all remember the concept of the Golden Mean. Even in Greece, perhaps not as far advanced as Persia, particular relationships between the large triangle, let's say, and the small triangle were known to produce feelings and emotions from those who experienced the Golden Mean. To move then to sound, the vibrations present in the high-pitched 'e' sound and the lower-pitched 'ah' sound are quite independent of anything in the human consciousness. They impinge on consciousness, and the study of magic in poetry directs itself to the families that these sounds make up and what the harmonies between them, when set up, do to us below the level of our conscious perception. In writing a poem, we are not honoring our grandfathers or our grandmothers or our own ability to make up fresh metaphors so much as honoring the actual sounds e, ah, oh, oi, im, in ar, er. There are perhaps 70 of these root sounds in English. Each poet usually chooses without intending to five or six of those sounds, and we recognize the oral mood of the poems through the constant repetition of those sounds. The sound 'ar,' for example, gives great psychic concentration to the poems in *Lord Weary's Castle.* Wallace Stevens loves 'en' and 'in' especially.

> The trade-wind jingles the rings in the nets around the racks
>   by the docks on Indian River.

If we can say that we look straight ahead when we try to say our thoughts clearly, and that we look down when we urge images to come up from whatever place below us they love to be, then we could say that when we honor sounds and encourage them to come into the poem, we close our eyes and look swiftly to the side. There is some teasing of the whole issue of truth and discourse when we begin to honor these strange vibrations that float far beyond the human soul. We are not so much truthful as playful when we look to the side. We are not so much thoughtful as cunning, and the magic comes in because each of these sounds is like a note on the clarinet or the sitar, and when we close our eyes and look to the side, we are asking impersonal tunes to enter the poem, and at that moment we may be both out of our mind and out of our soul.

Michelle Boisseau

Against the Muse

Go down to the stream and dip your rosebud
        fingernails among the fish flickering
          like earrings in a roomful
of dancers, go down to that stream,
those neoclassical waters
            where the humming of houseboys
  beating laundry with willow sticks
      frames you like a really good haircut,
go down to that stream, take your gold
sandals with you and leave my rivers alone.

       I don't know what these slumped roofs
are along the banks,
      just the way I like it,
  so discouraged-looking at first I can't tell
if they're abandoned barns or apartment houses,
the yellow kitchen clock, the strip of garden
       with a view of the 5:08 and the 10:40
    that hardly come around anymore,
and the barges unbraiding the muddy water
    rattle with coal raked out of my head.

I'm tired of them always inviting you
       as soon as a basket appears
   without a load of apricots
or canaries. Even if they slapped you together
      with creek mud instead of blue foam
        and took some plastic drinking straws
         instead of reeds to blow you up,
   they'd still dress you in wafting stuff
      so all the black ties and the bartender
out on the terrace would turn to see the wonder.
    A little breeze comes up and your frock
flaps about you, fine feathers
      though no bones to speak of,
wren, sparrow,

    and hardly the nerve
to move out of earshot, turn your back

on the great house,

> window dazzle, banked blossoms,
>
> Euclidian inclinations
>
> and come down here where the moss

can give you a good soaking and,

> if you hear them coming for you,

fill you with its messages.

The Muse's Sore Feet

WHENEVER I HEAR A LIVING PERSON TALK ABOUT HIS MUSE, I GET THE CREEPS. IN THE BEST OF all lights this notion of woman as Muse is kind of sweet. *Old-fashioned. Gentlemanly.* And I recognize the relationships between the Muse and rhetoric, the Muse and Mariolatry, courtly love, and sex.

It still gives me the creeps, this making amends for disenfranchisement by claiming that the disempowered wield true (and, naturally, *hidden*) power, that the voiceless inspire the voiced, that behind every great man . . . is an angel in the parlor who inspires and seduces, who gently reminds the weary warrior to keep his feet off the furniture. I see Beatrice, Laura, Penelope Devereaux aching in stiletto heels, tripping over their diaphanous gowns, and I want to tell them to wake up.

If the Muse stays true to the ideal, she's hardly human (best if she dies young like Beatrice). If she steps off the pearly path, like Penelope Devereaux (Sidney's Stella), woe to her. A story floated around when I was in graduate school that one of the Renaissance professors had once rejected a student's proposal to write on Penelope Devereaux (Sidney's Stella) because, he explained, that woman was a whore (for she left her lout of a husband for another man—one she spent the rest of her life with).

But wait, if a woman takes a man for a Muse, is the score even? Poetry's version of *Playgirl*? Hardly appealing. Why can't we give our own imaginations credit instead of laying the burden of inspiration on some other, on cruel chaste ladies, or Adonises, or almond-eyed extraterrestrials?

Last year when two English practical jokers were discovered to be the real source of the crop circles that were appearing mysteriously in the fields of southern England, I listened to people on NPR bemoan the discovery. Some people were even weeping. They had wanted space aliens, angels, druids, God—anything but humans to have made these other-worldly signs.

The human boldness was precisely what appealed to me: two men, in their sixties, had been trampling around under the stars, knocking huge, meaningless geometric figures into the grain just to see what people would make of them. What a great metaphor for human desire, for the creation of rites, religions, poetry, art, the stories we've concocted from random clusters of stars in the skies.

What did David Chorley and Douglas Bower use to create these circles believers hoped were landing pads for flying saucers? A four-foot plank, a ball of string and a baseball hat, its visor threaded to serve as a sighter. It reminds me of that famous response of Faulkner's. When he was asked what it takes to be a writer, he answered, "A pencil."

See Spot Run

The children of this storyville town
will change two pages of history
today is Monday 1968, late

The afternoon is raining fire hoses
and white riot helmets
lined up like a bowling alley
behind the grocery store's colored waiting room sign.

At the news stands and on the front page
of every television station, Walter Cronkite
is burning down the city
one block at a time. We are throwing bricks
through car windows.

Where is God
today is Monday, the afternoon of 1968, late.
The lower Eastside is burning
dogs in the name of sociology and other soap opera lies
disguised in free lunch boxes

handed out to a second grade school house
we are not allowed to come inside
but I'm here anyway.

Good morning boys and girls, good afternoon.
I'm Mr. Braggs and I'm your sub today.
Please take out your books.
Turn to pages 6 and 7
rip them out.
There is no Dick.
There is no Jane.
And Spot ain't nothing but a place
where the First Baptist of Birmingham used to be.

I HAVE COME TO UNDERSTAND THAT POETRY IS A PENCIL, A PENCIL SHARPENED TOO MANY times, nothing more. The straight grey suits of Macintosh and IBM are not poets; they can never be. Poetry is Bishop and Berryman twisted into wood painted yellow as a bus load of first graders on the first day of school. Poetry is down there in the early years, down at the root of things. Miklos Radnoti said, "I am the root of myself now, living among the worms. This poem is written down there." Every poem is written down there where the pencil makes love to the page.

I live at the root, I teach to stay alive, and I teach because, in spite of all, I love. One has to love. Perhaps occasion often finds me eating books of poetry for breakfast and novels for dinner over red Italian wine and candle light. Yes, I can be romantic. Perhaps I know that God will be in every poem I read this semester. And I know the semester will speak back to only a couple of them. Perhaps I am a fool for believing that the hand is smarter than the eye and the pencil speaks in many tongues. Perhaps next semester I will teach Modern Dance in Poetry 376 and sit back and delight in students slow dancing in soft tennis shoes and software. Perhaps I'll learn a step or two and they may learn to eat Chinese with pencils.

Ars Poetica

Here I am again, two stories up making a little peace
at the level of the trees—the Cherimoya and Chinese Elm,
Podocarpus and Digger Pine—pointing out the air's thin hands
as they twist Italian cypress into wicks, into green torches
touching off the blue.
                         And though I can tell cobalt blooms
of ceanothus from sky-pale plumbago, it's a little thing I do,
favorably disposed as we are to light, like the flaming nasturtiums
or the fragrant frangipani.
                         To open to something on its own terms,
to speak its name, is a good place to start up the ladder of desire—
and so, when asked, I say I do this to take advantage of everything
I don't fully know, to take in equally the self-satisfaction of clouds,
the almost perfect sorrow of rain, given the light's sealed lip,
given the old need to account for ourselves under the sun.

*

Scientists scrape down strata, through the calcification of time,
past a galaxy of shells, to star-silt, coal, and pinpoint
the ash of dinosaurs, the final days when creatures last lumbered
beside the palm trees, choking to death on the cold and dark.

It is a little thing we do, but what to make of these shed skins?
Surely we can learn from bones the dull lessons that would soon quit
our every breath, now that we can undo it all, take everything back
down to that first echo, the first disassembled dust?
                         Here I have it
otherwise a while, and take time to commend our orchard oriole,
the rogue pack of wrens picking apart the verbena, or the young cat
as she steals onto the roof of the storage shed for a better view—
how attentive they all are, how sure and sudden in their lives . . .

*

At 7 or 8, behind schoolrooms during lunch, I admired the windy lace
of acacias and lay among wild fennel and ivy locked into the anonymity
of the air, spelling out the silky progress of clouds. And I was not
thinking then of angels or of the shapes of beasts, but of the slow drift
of time keeping its counsel above me—the cataracts of light through limbs
revealing such riches as there were while we held onto our small place,
glorious and indifferent among the weeds.
                         Why do you do what you do?
is a question raised each time evening empties itself of light,
each time the sky rehearses its arpeggio of stars and signals you

to assume your place with or without some small verse of hope a life
might add up to.

        The world is equally at a loss, but there you are—
you can take up its troubles, its bundle of sticks, you can turn away
forsaking even the wind's mute prayer—or you can praise it beyond
all your means. There are few choices, and no matter what you choose
to love it is a little thing you do. So after a time there is no reason
not to wear your heart out on these white sleeves . . .

AS A YOUNG WRITER, I WAS TAKEN WITH A NUMBER OF ARS POETICA POEMS—MARIANNE
Moore's, Archibald MacLeish's, Wallace Stevens', and William Carlos Williams'. I liked the
way they broke with a stiff tradition and had their say, made more modern and democra-
tic, as well as more imaginative, claims for poetry. And although MacLeish's poem is often
remembered for its last two manifesto-like lines, I liked best the exact translation of desire
and mortality into images which gave an eloquent and concrete voice to the ineffable.

Then there were James Wright's and Charles Wright's ars poeticas. The former a
sequence of narrative vignettes mixed with lyric passages which combined so much right-
eous anger and tenderness, which spoke so directly it seemed perfect and impossible. The
latter, an evocation of the metaphysical grounded in the physical, in the heart of the writer
writing, a visionary energy and lyric hymn to the art. Each of these poems embodied a
different but equally compelling grace. Some of our best poets were saying, it seemed to
me, more memorably and directly than ever and with original craft, what they really
believed and felt.

So I went at my own poem from envy, coveting much. A youthful arrogance had me
thinking I too could say, with beauty, how important this was. I tried a number of times
and failed. I was not experienced enough to really know what I wanted to say, nor had I
the skill to handle the subject matter had I discovered it.

After I had been teaching several years, a graduate student at a reception for a visit-
ing poet asked me why I wrote poetry. She was deciding between writing fiction or poet-
ry and poetry seemed more marginal. The first image that came to mind by way of
response was a scene from early school days, eating lunch with friends in back of the class-
rooms, sitting among the acacias, wild ivy, and fennel as the few clouds held above the
foothills. I said I guessed I was trying to stop time, to hold on to moments like that. Not
a particularly memorable or motivating answer but an honest and spontaneous one, and
now, in retrospect, an accurate one.

Years later, trying to get back into a regular writing rhythm, I told myself to try and
remember what it was I used to obsess about before the burnout of a teaching load that
left me blank for the first weeks of summer. After a few days, I was working on a draft
with three subjects whose only connection was that they were my old obsessions—
Nature, the rich language of the flora and fauna in my home; the new cosmology and data
from science about the universe; and some clear moments from childhood. I thought
back to the time I'd tried to answer the question about why I wrote poetry and saw that
this might be my ars poetica. I'd published a few books by that point and had begun to
realize that what I was doing was not going to matter much, and so I had better just please
myself. I knew I was up against poems that would easily outdistance my effort, but I
stayed with my interests, my old obsessions and sources, and made a poem that, howev-
er modestly, I hoped would sing a little at the back of this choir.

The Big Money

I'm watching *Superman III* on my 19″ Sony Trinitron
which I bought along with other objects after receiving
money from the National Endowment for the Arts.
And a stereo, too, some Nike running shoes,
two new JBL speakers, and a Seiko watch.
And a boat, I have a boat out back, a bass boat.
I listen hard to the news, to hog futures and cash grains,
because the government can take it all back.
And I listen for static,
because you can get cheated. I remember once,
for two weeks, I saved lunch money to buy a gun,
because what if someone came up to me and
wanted my lunch money? Jimmy Olsen is
hanging on to a building he can't hold on to
much longer. He once had a poem in *Poetry* magazine.
Later he became Jimmy Olsen and now
he writes libretti for the big money.
I think we greedy ones must break
Superman's heart. I study the cape unfurled
like a flag of the commonwealth, his easy
offhand heroic stare, but wait . . . !
I bought a Pekinese. And he won't bark.
He lies and licks himself like any dog.
Like any old hound who eats and drinks
and sleeps under the Indian-giver sun
on any given day in the Metropolis.

WHO WAS IT WHO SAID TURN DOWN NO GRANT MONEY? THIS IS LESS AN ARS POETICA THAN A low-class, not very direct swipe at careerism. It would be catastrophic for art to appreciate patronage too solemnly since it must threaten it too. The beginning of this poem celebrates Mammon as it were. (Most people who aren't used to money buy things with it.) Then it includes an incident that happens to be true. Jimmy Olsen (real name, Jack Larson) really did publish a poem in *Poetry*, right there beside Joyce Kilmer's "Trees," and now he's a flourishing librettist. The gun I wanted to buy was a combination BB/pellet pistol.

The title (suggested to me by Michael Heffernan) of my second book derives from this poem's last line. It also may be worth noting that Chris Buckley received an NEA the same year I did, as did Wayne Dodd, who built a writing studio which he called "Big Money Cabin." So my poem has already gained a certain currency.

The Impossible Indispensability of
the Ars Poetica

But of course the poem is not an assertion. Do you see? When I wrote
That all my poems over the long years before I met you made you come true,
And that the poems for you since then have made you in yourself become
      more true,
I did not mean that the poems created or invented you. How many have
      foundered
In that sargasso! No, what I have been trying to say
Is that neither of the quaint immemorial views of poetry is adequate for us.
A poem is not an expression, nor is it an object. Yet it somewhat partakes of
      both. What a poem is
Is never to be known, for which I have learned to be grateful. But the aspect
      in which I see my own
Is as the act of love. The poem is a gift, a bestowal.
The poem is for us what instinct is for animals, a continuing and chiefly
      unthought corroboration of essence
(Though thought, ours and the animals', is still useful).
Why otherwise is the earliest always the most important, the formative? The
      Iliad, the Odyssey, the Book of Genesis,
These were acts of love, I mean deeply felt gestures, which continuously
      bestow upon us
What we are. And if I do not know which poem of mine
Was my earliest gift to you,
Except that it had to have been written about someone else,
Nevertheless it was the gesture accruing value to you, your essence, while
      you were still a child, and thereafter
Across all these years. And see how much
Has come from that first sonnet after our loving began, the one
That was a kiss, a gift, a bestowal. This is the paradigm of fecundity. I think
      the poem is not
Transparent, as some have said, nor a looking-glass, as some have also said,
Yet it has almost the quality of disappearance
In its cage of visibility. It disperses among the words. It is a fluidity, a vapor,
      of love.
This, the instinctual, is what caused me to write "Do you see?" instead of
      "Don't you see?" in the first line
Of this poem, this loving treatise, which is what gives away the poem
And gives it all to you.

THE IDEA IN MY POEM, VIZ. THAT HUMAN LOVING IS WHAT GIVES US ALL RECOGNITION AND value, is implicit in many works of the mid-century secular existentialist writers, especially Sartre's *Being and Nothingness*, but it comes particularly from the first chapter of *The Nature of Love*, by Irving Singer (New York, 1966), a book that has been important to me. The poem attempts to assimilate this idea to a theory of poetry, and I don't think this is mere sentimentalism. All poetry is—or should be—written in love of the world. All poetry is in some sense erotic. The act of love, as opposed to lust, and the act of the imagination, as opposed to technological invention, occupy the same area of human consciousness. They are acts of mutuality and exchange, from which all participants derive value and understanding, and hence they are indispensable. Yet they are human endeavors too, and always contain the germ of their own impossibility and failure, which is the topic of other poems and essays I have written.

Lucille Clifton

here yet be dragons

so many languages have fallen
off of the edge of the world
into the dragon's mouth.   some

where there be monsters whose teeth
are sharp and sparkle with lost

people.   lost poems   who
among us can imagine ourselves
unimagined?   who

among us can speak with so fragile
tongue and remain proud?

Judith Ortiz Cofer

Letter from My Mother in Spanish

She writes to me as if we still shared
the same language. The page
a laden sky, filled with flying letters
suspended just above the lines
like blackbirds on the horizon;
the accents—something smaller
they are pursuing.

                  She says:
after a lifetime of tending to people,
my grandmother is obsessed
with useless endeavors—raising fat hens
she refuses to eat, letting them live
until their feathers droop and drag
on the dirt, like the hems
of slovenly women.

           "Listen,"
she writes, forgetting that the words
cannot pull me by the elbow, "she will not pick
the roses she grows, so that walking
through her garden is like following a whore—
the smell chokes you; makes you
want to loosen your dress.

        "She fills her house with old things:
baby pictures she misnames, mistaking me
for you, undoing the generations; yellowed ads
for beauty products and clothes; headlines
from the War; her last child's obituary—
the one who never tasted sugar,
then he died of something simple.

          "She has no use now
for those of us who survived. Your aunts
and I take turns at her side, but if we burn
a light in the dark rooms she prefers,
she covers her face as if ashamed.
If we dust the picture-frames, she claims
we are trying to erase the past.

"Daughter, *basta.* Enough for now."

I read her letter aloud, for the sound
of Spanish, and it becomes a Kyrie,
a litany in a mass for the dead.
I take each vowel on my tongue.
La abuela, brings tears to my eyes
like incense; *la muerte,*
sticks in my throat like ashes.

Her blessing is a row of black crosses
on a white field.

Some Spanish Words

PALABRAS: I CAME TO WRITING BY BEING CURIOUS ABOUT THE SECRET MEANINGS OF WORDS, *palabras* that were spoken in my presence in two languages and not always explained. I began to think about writing as I heard the stories told by my grandmother and other women in my family. At some point I took note of the performance of language, learned to appreciate the subtleties of emphasis, tone, placement of words; of images called forth by carefully selected words. Before I knew terms like metaphor or analogy, I heard people being compared to birds, beasts of burden, rocks and mountains. I listened carefully as the women drew comparisons between their lives and the way of the cross, and even to Calvary. "*¡Que Calvario!*" one of them would exclaim after recounting her hardships—as a good Catholic girl I had no trouble making the connection. I heard key words of a woman's *vida* spoken with force and resonance: *La sangre, la muerte, el amor.* These syllables would later come to me as I faced the page like tiny messengers from the past, bearing images.

La abuela, la muerte: My muse is an old island woman who speaks in parables, in riddles, in the voice of my grandmother. It is la abuela's voice that I hear when I train my mind's telescope on early memories. La abuela saw everything, knows what really happened. She reveals the truth to me in the coded language of symbols. La abuela as my muse is immortal. Or at least, she will live for as long as I believe in her power. In less mystical terms, la abuela is my connection to my first language, my native land, and my childhood—the stuff of many of my poems.

My human abuela, who really did teach me about the power of words, is old, and will like all mortals, die. In my poem, my mother writes to tell me that my abuela is withdrawing from "reality" into her own world of memories. She fears that this is the beginning of the end for a woman known for her strength, her sharp intelligence, and a life dedicated to the service of a large family. I wrote the poem as a sort of preparation for the inevitable disappearance of a powerful physical presence in my life. I will have to accept the fact that one day, perhaps soon, I will get the letter from my mother in Spanish in which I will read *la abuela, la muerte* in one sentence. In writing the poem I discovered a connection between my description of la abuela collecting the tokens of her life and what I do as a poet. The "useless things" I name represent *la vida* to her: lost youth, strength and beauty, memories of a war—condensed for her in a child's obituary—and the family photographs, now all blending in her mind as one. As she loses her vitality, the past becomes more important to hold on to: these objects are evidence of having lived. Her greatest fear is that the memories will be erased, and with it her life. Like la abuela, I hoard artifacts; like her I struggle to put the fragments together in patterns that means *la vida.* This act of remembering triggers and sometimes *is* the poem to me.

The River

That fear inside me all this time,
like chicken wire I could almost see through to,
turns out to be just a childhood,
fully formed, but boyish,
wrapped in a blanket
within shouting distance
of the house he grew up in.
It's 3 o'clock in the morning,
the inside of black, blacker, even
than the hair of the woman he'll later marry.
But what he wants now
is to be swallowed whole by sleep—
to sleep and add the sound of his breathing
to all the night sounds around him.
He has yet to realize his family
is part of the world and so he has renounced
with it the world and so he is sleeping
beside the night, not with it. He cannot
throw his leg over the night anymore
than he can throw his leg over himself,
the sound of black does not yet run through him,
and no matter how black his sleeves,
the pale palms of his hands remind him
he is himself still, separate.
That stone in the brook,
like the knuckle of a hand—
is the river in it
the way he wants to be in someone?
He needs to think that,
splitting the stone, he would find its center
damp as the very late or very early mist
that finds its way into the heart and dissolves
its boundaries. He does not yet know
the mist takes its shape from the emptiness
of the world, it begins there
between trees and houses,
in the margins of singularity
that allow us to see each other.
The mist would mean nothing were the world whole,
yet the world is whole because of the mist,
and though I cannot see the boy any longer,
and though he seems no more to me
than a log softened by flame,
the rock, at its heart,
is wet with the river,
and the river flowing more slowly through rock,
is nonetheless a river for that.

It's ironic that I think of "The River" as a poem that represents an important part of my aesthetic; ironic, because in terms of the devices and conventions it employs, it doesn't seem to. There's none of the tragi-comic, conversational irony that my poems are often steeped in. There's no radical synthesis of disparate tones. It doesn't depend on anecdote and it moves in a fluid, rather than fractured, way through a fairly limited time frame and but one schematically rendered dramatic setting. The level of diction seems almost absurdly simple and consistent, especially considering that even though its imagery is natural, the poem is primarily made up of abstract statements and straight-forward, omniscient observations. The poem seems to have a definite point, even though it couches itself in a dualistic, archetypical atmosphere. I suppose I hope that the plain language, and the constant repetition of it, reinforce the child-like nature of the subject matter, while simultaneously undercutting the "philosophical" or rational nature of the poem's construct. And in this sense, the poem does fall into line with my usual M.O. — make it look casual and heartfelt to disguise the fact I'm totally enamored of ideas and the safety zone between the world of my head and the world of actuality.

Which, of course, is what the poem may be really about. If it is anything, it is a momentary embrace of the mystery inherent in the process of self-actualization; a disguised direct address begging forgiveness for those tendencies toward insularity and over-intellectualization. It is, I hope, a celebration of the difficulties of selfhood—whatever it is in us that calls us to greater awareness of our selves and the world of selves of which we are a part—whatever it is that calls us to write poems.

Westering

They tell me to write about the West,
about mountains, rivers, arroyos.
I take a feather from my pocket,
write the wheat's waving across the sky.

They tell me to write about
the frontier, about cabins and Indian wars.
I take a willow leaf from the lake
and each period is a fish eye
dotting the rain, each comma a wet stem.

They tell me to write about
the corral, cowboys and cattle.
They stand there waiting.
Here beside the water I wait too
to catch myself as I watch
the bird in the willow, the fish.

Under me I feel the world's wheels
grinding and above me the Peruvian sky
slides into view as it passes on
toward the south and the Andes.

And I a western woman write:
They tell me to write about place.
So I travel in a circle,
always and ever heading west.

IF IT IS TRUE, AS NORTHROP FRYE HAS SAID, THAT "POETS NO LONGER IMITATE THE ACTIONS OF gods or heroes, or allegorical representatives of ideal virtues, or states of *bourgeois* well-being, or intense and exciting states of subjective feeling: they imitate the untidy, shabby, incoherent pattern of everyday life as it is," then it is hard to see how poetry can help but be political. But poetry also requires freedom.

I think of Cesar Vallejo and his struggle to create his poems free of any dogma—political or aesthetic. My ideal is to sit down to write my poem and be able to erase my consciousness of what poetry *should* be or do; then I could begin again at the beginning and might be able, as Alice recommended, to go on until I came to the end. Whatever it might be.

Robert Dana

In the Gardens of Fabulous Desire

39, west of Hollandale,
a sharp, backward curve
and you miss it, the small
house set in deep shade;
lion and swan and tower
rising from the burnt grass.
No scene from childhood,
unless yours, like mine,
was a long, bad dream.
When you kill your engine
and step down in the rutted
gravel, and pass finally
under the dark pines,
you'll feel the hair lift
on your scalp a little,
absent eyes watching
from behind dimity curtains
brittle with dust and sun.
But the cheesemaker whose
house this was—grey stucco
studded with bits of bottle
glass, pastel Fiestaware,
fragments of mirror—he's
dead now. His woman, gone.
Sons moved on to Sheboygan
or Monroe. Nothing left
but this house and its gardens
of fabulous desire. Blond
Snow White, breasts
swelling under her scallop-
shell bodice. The Viking
in his griffin-prowed skiff,
beached and listing, summer
after summer, further
into the glacial earth. It
may come to you like the cry
of children playing out
of sight across a green ravine.

Or distant as the jumble
of sleepy bees, hum of flies,
gorged with musky blackberries
beyond the milkhouse—what
are our calloused hands,
leaky bladders, and bad backs,
but drunken song? Our ruined
faces, but work? And you
may think if you could get
the words to ring down
right, like Neptune's Wheel,
noun, verb; noun, verb;
the clown under his pointed
cap, the owl, the boy reading,
noun, verb—this whole
Calliope of crumbling dream
would wheeze again, whirl
and sing in the wild heat
and stagger of these weeds.

The Calliope In the Garden

WRITING A POEM, EVEN A MODERATELY SUCCESSFUL ONE, IS AN ACT AKIN TO MAGIC. IT INVOLVES a kind of occult knowledge of how language works or might be made to. So being asked to write about it is like someone in the dugout mentioning you have a no-hitter going just before you walk out to face the last three batters in the top of the ninth. Writers of my stripe are as superstitious as baseball players or witch doctors. And when the secret subject is broached, the air turns the color of dread.

When I think of "In the Gardens of Fabulous Desire," and occasionally I do, I think of it as my "Sailing to Byzantium." And I think of how, perhaps oddly, Yeats has been a benchmark of passion and craftsmanship for me for a very long time. At first, consciously; later, unconsciously.

I say "oddly," because most of my contemporaries, and certainly most younger American male poets, cue on Whitman or Williams. Perhaps Yeats' influence came into my work via the work of Robert Lowell, one of my early teachers. Although it's more likely, I think, that as a young man just escaped from the cloying philistinism of a 1930s Boston Irish Catholic background, my ear was especially attuned to the fierce lyricism of certain of Yeats' poems. In fact, one of my earliest published poems, "For Sister Mary Apolline," published in *Poetry* in 1957, was a deliberate imitation, formally, of "Among Schoolchildren," and the actual music of a poem is still an important consideration for me.

"In the Gardens of Fabulous Desire," written thirty years later, is not a conscious imitation of any Yeats poem, of course. And it wasn't until long after I finished the poem that I began to sense the kinship. Both poems are about youth and age, about mortality and transcendence, about "the artifice of eternity." Both poems are concerned with the "fabulous." "Once out of nature I shall never take/ My bodily form from any natural thing,/ But such a form as Grecian goldsmiths make...."

We live in an age of the mundane. A Warhol world where what little glory there is lasts about ten minutes, and Grecian goldsmiths have long since gone the way of Ari and Jackie; what happens when you and your wife are driving backcountry blacktop for the scenery and to avoid the sleep-inducing boredom of the freeway. Around a tight little curve, there it is. And then it's gone. But it *was* there, wasn't it? You find a farmyard driveway a mile further on and turn the car around.

The place is eerie. It's charged ground. There's no one in the house, and there hasn't been for a long time. The blackberries behind the unused milkhouse are huge and wild and sweet. I can still taste them as I write this. And I see, in retrospect, that every single important icon and detail in the poem was immediately and physically present during this first encounter. I knew this was a place where lives had been lived so banal and strange that they had required monuments. I also knew immediately that I would write about this place and these people, that it would not be soon, and that I didn't know exactly what form the writing would take. My wife and I continued to prowl and scrutinize and photograph, and then drove on to Mineral Point to find out whatever there was to find out. I didn't write the poem that year. Or even the next. I've always been slow. I still didn't understand what I was looking at.

Over the next four or five years, we stopped by twice more, en route home from salmon fishing expeditions in northern Wisconsin, taking photographs each time. Each time, another of the crude sculptures had tumbled into the grass or been vandalized or had passed into an advanced state of decay. And each time, as I peered through the dusty windows of the little house into a room where nothing had moved or been moved during the intervening years, I would try again to enter the mood that had turned a man who'd made cheese into a folk artist of urgency and surpassing strangeness. To connect with the human being who had turned his lawn into a museum to whimsy and nightmare, and something more.

*

For me, writing is an act of discovery.

Some events, some people, are, for me, so charged with passionate complexity, that only the slow process of verbalizing them on paper allows me any measure of understanding. I start with the local, usually, trying to get it factually right, then follow where the words and the music lead.

For example, Highway 39. That's a quantitative and geographic fact. A "hard" fact, as they say. Check a Wisconsin map. It's there. I really never fully understood the importance this number printed as a number has for this poem, until the poem was being translated into Italian. The translator rendered the number as a word, "trentanovisima." When I had lived uneasily with this version of it for a few days, I realized that the numbers mark the margin of common reality in the poem, distinguish it from a landscape transformed by art and dream and fable. The numbers also mark the crossing point between the two worlds, linking them. Perhaps so the traveller may find his way back to the world of hard fact.

The poem moves quickly on then to the fabled world of "lion and swan and tower," images that suggest, at first, childhood and innocence. But the "innocence" of both childhood and fable is often short-lived. The best fables, "Hansel and Gretel," for instance, often have about them, like the childhoods of some of us, the qualities of a "bad dream," plots that turn on the presence of evil, cruelty, and death. Such fables are not entirely unlike the reality of the poem where you can "kill" even your engine; where you may look in vain for the absent artist and find only the monuments, the "works" of his "fabulous desire." For another, a better reality? Permanence? Immortality?

Yeats, in 1927, had faith in the redeeming power of art. He would become the golden bird on a golden bough, the permanent and prophetic singer "Of what is past, or passing, or to come." The writer of "In the Gardens of Fabulous Desire" has no such faith.

Perhaps the tragedy and the triumph of this poem viewed as an ars poetica is that its core is more aesthetic than didactic. The aesthetic, Borges tells us, involves the "imminence of a revelation which does not occur." "Certain places," he says, "try to tell us something, or have said something we should not have missed, or are about to say something." All prophecy has proven false in this century, and revelation the work of chauvinists and con artists. Imminence is all we have. Perhaps all we have ever had.

Thus, whatever the details of this poem say about life and art can only be apprehended and expressed aslant; indirectly and, therefore, incompletely. Because, like the original experience, the sum of its mute detail is the vastly unspecific "cry of children . . . out of sight," or the "jumble" and "hum" of not quite articulate bees and flies, or as outcry and question: "what/are our calloused hands,/ . . . and bad backs,/ . . . Our ruined faces. . ."? Are they "drunken song" or "work"? Are "song" and "work" the same thing in the context of the poem? Is song, too, a "cry"? And do I mean by "drunken," ecstatic or drugged? In fact, the poem doesn't, I think, exclude any of these possibilities and remains, therefore, true to itself.

In its final dozen lines, the poem tries to redefine the question both it and the art of the cheesemaker seem to have been groping toward. Can art, either as sculpture or as speech ("noun, verb; noun verb;"), driven to the level of the fabulous by intensity of desire, transcend mortality? Can it redeem or compensate for or ennoble the indignities of age, and the physical labor that breaks the body? At first, ". . . Gardens. . ." might seem to confirm the Yeatsian view. The presence of Neptune and Calliope may seem to suggest god-like powers. But the language is very conditional: "you/may think *if you could* get/the words to ring down/right. . . ."

The poem, in fact, puts a hard, skeptical spin on the traditional theme. The redemption and immortality both the poet and the sculptor have sought in the past to achieve through skills raised to the level of the magical, they can, in fact, no longer achieve. They never really could. In both the poem and in everyday reality, Neptune and Calliope are crumbling into dust. Indeed, this poem seems to say all our lives are neither more nor less than "crumbling dream": the cheesemaker's, the reader's, the writer's, the lives of children and flies and weeds. But against the inescapable "wheeze" and "stagger," against the final collapse into "glacial earth," there's the possibility of, if not immortality, at least honor through art.

Perhaps dream is all, the poem seems to suggest. Perhaps the work done, no matter how mundane or how grand, is the song and the dance; and the lines and scars we bear from it, dignity. And perhaps poetry honors this wild dream of living.

Ars Poetica

At last, her hands are not shaking.
Finally, her eyes are dry.
She thinks of the dead
calmly, without terror.
She thinks of paintings and history
to remind herself how small
and insignificant
her tragedies are, how bad
they might have been.

The painter's parents
died at Dachau,
and his famous picture
shows them walking away
older than they ever were,
worn-out and gray, trudging
up a hillside forever.

She likes the painting
because its story
cannot change, cannot
continue to the nocturnal round-up,
the trains of terrified families
passing through the night.
In the painting, the dead
are walking up a mountain
forever. They will not get cold
or hungry or any older.
They will not die.

She likes to imagine
the painter at his easel,
temporarily relieved
of his tragic history
and personal pain.

For a short while, he had only
a *task*: combining color
on the palette;
a *problem*: how thickly
to apply the paint.
His tragedy eventually became a picture
—a beautiful picture.
Then someone bought it from him
and took it away.

On the Unbearable

THE UNBEARABLE IS WHAT I MOST OFTEN WRITE ABOUT, I SUPPOSE, AND IN THIS POEM, the unbearable is the emotion that I felt, almost fifteen years ago, upon seeing a reproduction of Henry Koerner's "My Parents," painted in 1946-47. Koerner's parents, from whom he was separated during World War II, died in a Nazi concentration camp. As I recall the story that the painter once told about this painting, he revisited the site of his former home in Europe after the war only to find it destroyed by bombing. In the ruins, he spied some fragment of women's clothing that he remembered as having once belonged to his mother. The loss of his parents and his traumatic experience at their ruined home resulted in "My Parents," an eerie, surrealistic depiction of two elderly people, walking, backs toward the viewer, up an incline. The colors are all gold, yellow, brown; the mood is more somber and mysterious than it is elegiac, as if Koerner is trying to understand some great and terrifying mystery. The mystery is the one that has wrenched him from his parents, depriving him of any future with them, and consigning them to an eternity together in their sadness that he can never understand, and can never enter. Because of the text that accompanied the reproduction I saw, the painting had—and still has in my imagination, although I have not seen it for a decade—a devastatingly effective way of bringing together the worlds of both private and public catastrophes. The collision of historical fact and personal pain felt unbearable to me, and, yet, that collision, which is a constant in our world, *must* be borne, mustn't it? if we are to survive. More than anything else, the painting reminds me that human beings cannot be abstracted, cannot be consigned to "the six million dead," the "Bosnian Muslims," the "antebellum slaves," or any other unbearable part of our history we wish to tidy up or simply just forget about.

My poem imagines the painting of the picture and ponders some of the emotional benefits that transferring the tragedy to canvas might have had for the artist. In particular, it focuses on the indescribable, magical moment of creation that is probably a large part of what keeps people writing and painting—that endlessly suspended moment when time disappears as words get spoken and paint makes shapes. After that process is concluded, I am always somehow finished with the poem as it is on the page. In order to bring it to life again, I need the participation of another. Someone like you, reading this poem, who, in an act of exchange, will "buy it" from me and "take it away." My unbearable becomes our unbearable; together, as writer and reader, we will acknowledge it, specify it, and spread the news. In that act of communion, it is my hope that we lessen the future occurrence of all things unbearable.

The Fish Tank

I sit watching TV and a parade
of pills, bottles, soaps and blades punishes
but gives me dreams. Sometimes the dreams invade

my waking hours and I live on the edge of things
where the curtains puff with meaning, the chairs
hold themselves with dignity and the wings

of the ebony table are resilient
with a power which they won't use. The things
I see are tense, disciplined and sapient.

I scoop up pebbles from the goldfish tank.
I touch them for their hardness. One is clouded
and glazed like a dead eyeball that's gone blank

with nothing to see. I see the fish caught there
in the water, their veins shot with stone, the
barbeled mouths turned up pulsing at the air.

WHEN I FIRST BEGAN TO WRITE POEMS SERIOUSLY, I WAS READING WILLIAM CARLOS WILLIAMS.
Williams and other contemporary American poets were saying that the iamb came from
what it was to be European and was incapable of measuring a freer American experience.
American poets should not employ the traditional meters. Out of curiosity I began to
compose poems in accentual syllabics as though this were a kind of forbidden fruit and
with this came a number of surprising discoveries.

I soon began to see, for example, how the iamb had the power to press itself more
deeply into memory and it was, for me, more resonant. Metrical composition became
experimental. I began to see and feel firsthand what it could do. The poem, "The Fish
Tank," one of my earliest poems, is a case in point. It is written in rhymed three-line stan-
zas. The meter and the rhyme helped me to say what I unconsciously believed. It is
unlikely I would have revealed these values to myself without them.

These values have more than aesthetic application, but I began this poem simply
with the idea that I would take things around me, familiar things and use them in a
poem. So I began.

Before I finished the first stanza I felt a need to alter a context which seemed too
mundane and so I introduced dream work. This gave me a chance to impart to the imag-
ined things around me subjective qualities. The necessity to rhyme 'things' gave me 'wings'
with its connotations of flight and freedom in a context of classical restraint. 'Resilient'
gave me 'sapient,' a word which I would not have used otherwise. And so rhyme began to
exert its imaginative capabilities to draw from the subconscious and to shape.

But beneath all this is a loose accentual syllabic meter, more syllabic than accentual
in this case. The rhythms of this meter are close to pentameter and sometimes elevate
and sometimes give an otherwise prosaic experience a kind of ritual connection to a larg-
er source of meaning. Consider

a parade
of pills, bottles, soaps and blades punishes
but gives me dreams. Sometimes the dreams invade

The slow movement of the iambs "but gives me dreams" is the beginning of a lyrical movement in this line which rises emotionally just above the merely real and imparts to this a kind of strangeness. This rhythm then symbolizes the way this particular voice, this sensibility, transforms what would be very ordinary.

Through this transformation comes a sense of meaning and the lines that find in restraint, control and clarity a kind of wisdom; but if the poem ended on this key sentence "The things/I see are tense, disciplined and sapient," it would be an incomplete poetic act, and in another way it would only constitute a part of the truth. For if clarity, restraint and control are pushed too far the thing alive becomes petrified and sterile and has a kind of death in life.

⟨⟨⟨⟩⟩⟩

Fred Dings

Redwing Blackbirds

This morning they came like the dying
reclaiming their old lives, delirious
with joy right on the seam of spring,
streaming in by the tattered thousands
like black leaves blowing back onto the trees.

But the homeless know what's expected by now,
and when the farmer fired into their body,
they rose all around me like trembling
black wounds gaping red at the shoulders,
a river of pain draining into the sky.

Tonight, as I look at the cold sky
and its flock of blue-white scars,
I can't yet turn from Orion's red star
whose trembling red light has travelled for years
to die now into any eyes that will hold it.

AT FIRST GLANCE, YOU SEE THREE STANZAS OF EQUAL LENGTH WITH LINES OF ROUGHLY EQUAL length. The poem, however, is not strictly metered nor are the lines end-rhymed. I choose instead a music that evolves within the necessities of the poem's "content," the way the form of a particular species of life will evolve in adaptation to the necessities of its environment. Also, I frequently prefer an imagistic density greater than what is commonly encountered in free verse poems. Generally speaking, I find a poem's intensity is proportionately increased, the way the temperature is increased in a closed cylinder of gas when the volume of the cylinder is reduced, creating closer proximity of the molecules and thus greater friction.

⟨⟨⟨⟩⟩⟩

Ars Poetica

Thirty miles to the only decent restaurant
was nothing, a blink
in the long dull stare of Wyoming.
Halfway there the unknown but terribly
important essayist yelled Stop!
I wanna be *in* this; and walked
fifteen yards onto the land
before sky bore down and he came running,
crying Jesus—there's nothing out there!

I once met an Australian novelist
who told me he never learned to cook
because it robbed creative energy.
What he wanted most was
to be mute; he stacked up pages;
he entered each day with an ax.

What I want is this poem to be small,
a ghost town
on the larger map of wills.
Then you can pencil me in as a hawk:
a traveling x-marks-the-spot.

I NEVER THOUGHT I'D FEEL THE URGE TO WRITE AN ARS POETICA . . . BUT, AS HENRI PIGEON
sings in *An American Tail,* "Never say never." My poem was a spontaneous outpouring, a
reaction to what I considered to be a cynical (or naive?) exercise another poet/professor
had assigned to a beginning poetry class: write your own ars poetica. Young writers, so
eager to believe in the possibility of "doing the right thing," so prone to making sweep-
ing esthetic pronouncements based on the haphazard reading lists of the undergraduate
curriculum—how could they be expected to come up with a philosophy of poetry? Why
would anyone want to encourage them to approach writing "from the top," as it were,
rather than to dive in up to the elbows?

My poem is meant to be an anti-ars poetica, one that shows how many of our beliefs
turn out to be metaphysical stances based on superstitious behavior. My "Ars Poetica" is
anecdotal because so much talk about writing these days is entertaining rather than
essential. In the last stanza, though, the poem manages to fool the poet. Against the
metaphorical backdrop of the Wild West (new frontiers!), the poet-as-hawk **does** assume
the robes of authority, though her pronouncement is a sly one, a warning to critics and
culture popes everywhere: Don't Fence Me In.

Of Politics, & Art

Here, on the farthest point of the peninsula
The winter storm
Off the Atlantic shook the schoolhouse.
Mrs. Whitimore, dying
Of tuberculosis, said it would be after dark
Before the snowplow and bus would reach us.

She read to us from Melville.

How in an almost calamitous moment
Of sea hunting
Some men in an open boat suddenly found themselves
At the still and protected center
Of a great herd of whales
Where all the females floated on their sides
While their young nursed there. The cold frightened whalers
Just stared into what they allowed
Was the ecstatic lapidary pond of a nursing cow's
One visible eyeball.
And they were at peace with themselves.

Today I listened to a woman say
That Melville *might*
Be taught in the next decade. Another woman asked, "And why not?"
The first responded, "Because there are
No women in his one novel."

And Mrs. Whitimore was now reading from the Psalms.
Coughing into her handkerchief. Snow above the windows.
There was a blue light on her face, breasts and arms.
Sometimes a whole civilization can by dying
Peacefully in one young woman, in a small heated room
With thirty children
Rapt, confident and listening to the pure
God rendering voice of a storm.

"Of Politics, & Art" began in draft and was abandoned. Years later it was taken up again, still just a memory of childhood, but something new had insinuated itself upon the poem—this new element was a fragment of dialogue that had drifted up a long hallway to me a week before. It altered the course of the original poem somewhat, and gave the poem its title. The reader will probably need to be reminded, as the poet was, that the word *rendering* applies to fat and whaling as well as to the nineteenth-century kit of chalk pastels. The poem, oddly enough, is absolutely accurate in its treatment of an experience from childhood. It is an homage to a great teacher.

How It Is

This is how it is—

One turns away
and walks out into the evening.
There is a white horse on the prairie, or a river
that slips away among dark rocks.

One speaks, or is about to speak,
not that it matters.

What matters is this—

It is evening.
I have been away a long time.
Something is singing in the grass.

"How It Is" GOES BACK A NUMBER OF YEARS. I WROTE IT AT A TIME WHEN I HAD GROWN WEARY of reading/writing poems that all too frequently consisted of occasions inflated with the helium of "significance" or, worse, were merely banal anecdotes fished up from the academic backwaters of W. C. Williams. I wanted a form that would be relatively austere, compressed, little given to ornamentation or elevated diction—a poem that allowed our silences to become essential parts of speech. I think of poets such as Machado or Louise Bogan, for example: poets different from each other, in important ways, yet writing poems in which an apparent simplicity of style is under great pressure being exerted from internal demands. Personal temperament, I suppose, has much to do with taste, and it is probably no accident that I find in such restraint the dignity and beauty I most often associate with the poems I love.

I don't wish to make excessive claims for my own poem. It provides little practical information for anyone setting out to write a poem. If it speaks of poetry, it speaks of process (how) rather than definition (what), of what is prior to rather that what is after. And because I often go for long periods of time without writing, it speaks also of renewal, of how the common particulars of the world may at times return us to what is wondrous and immediate and abundant.

To explain in prose, however, what I have tried to say in a poem is not my purpose, even if I could be trusted to know the truth. Perhaps, then, I can best speak of these matters indirectly: I imagine a good horn man—Ben Webster, say—in those moments just before he rides out onto the sounds that he hopes will sustain and lift up his solo. He listens to the others, listens as it all gets to moving so sweet and loose, and in his solitude he begins to fashion his first notes, which will be made of his own breath and of everything he's been given.

Music for Death

You are right. At death I might well desire both day and rest,

some calm place where light is stabilized on an arbor,

a table, green glasses, and damask. The taste is of earth and sunlight

tomatoes with folds at the blossom end and a large rough navel

with a bit of stem still attached, oil with basil

and lots of garlic, causing thirst for wine. And the music

to be played at my funeral must be the sound of the rosined bow

working against the wind, not old keys that are only echoes, but strange

gold in the beetle's click, a jay, a three color bird, a brown thrush,

their asides and intimations like the napkin songs

of great composers, written before the last bread and wine are gone.

"MUSIC FOR DEATH" WASN'T WRITTEN AS AN ARS POETICA, THOUGH TO DEFINE AN AESTHETIC or moral abstraction has become, of late, a preoccupation of mine in a series of eleven-line poems, poems quite close to this one in form and stance. The new poems, as well as this one, define more by example than by statement, and may become a sort of metaphoric equivalent for what is being talked about. A poem that does that is by nature one as much about the writing of itself as it is about its ostensible subject.

The poem acts out my poetics, or a portion of them. It acknowledges and is intimate with its audience in its seeming continuation of a dialogue. Its *music* is part natural and part formal, as is its tone, starting with "You are right" instead of the more colloquial "You're right." The three stresses introduced there occur several times in the poem as a rhythmic motif. It is an elegy of sorts, but a self-elegy, which ups the ante and certainly must seem to have potential for humor; irony in the lyric poem is always a pleasant surprise, is it not?

Art's spontaneity is featured in "the napkin songs/of the great composers." And the whole of the poem is given over to the sensual. Finally, the connection made between the natural world and art, of bird song and the wind—not forgetting the oils and colors and tomato stems—with generations of composers, who take inspiration from the natural world and write what they can write down quickly before all is lost, implies, is meant to imply, something about the relation between mortality and immortality and is meant to praise nature and the imagination. But the rest must be left to the reader.

Art Class

Let us begin with a simple line,
Drawn as a child would draw it,
To indicate the horizon,

More real than the real horizon,
Which is less than line,
Which is visible abstraction, a ratio.

The line ravishes the page with implications
Of white earth, white sky!

The horizon moves as we move,
making us feel central.
But the horizon is an empty shell—

Strange radius whose center is peripheral.
As the horizon draws us on, withdrawing,
The line draws us in,

Requiring further lines,
Engendering curves, verticals, diagonals,
Urging shades, shapes, figures. . . .

What should we place, in all good faith,
On the horizon? A stone?
An empty chair? A submarine?

Take your time. Take it easy.
The horizon will not stop abstracting us.

POETRY, IT'S OBVIOUS, REQUIRES NO COMMENT. AN ARS POETICA IS ALREADY, THEREFORE, a failure of character. To comment on an ars poetica would be a double failure to which, though now guilty, I am unwilling to admit.

Credo

My meaning passes like wild nightbirds
Whose cries are like the dew, risen
Or fallen, night's emanation, clear
Sayings of the unsystematized.

Clearer than crystal: plainer than day:
Simpler than absence when after hope
And memory—dream and empire—are blown
Away like cities we wake to the desert.

Doctrine has never sheltered this
Untamed belief that takes the whole
For its housing, heaven and earth and breath
And sleep, the undivided sphere.

BREWSTER GHISELIN'S "CREDO" IS NOT SO MUCH AN ARS POETICA AS AN ARS VITA—A PRIMER on the art of living, out of which poems emerge in the same inevitable fashion as catkins on a quaking aspen. What the poet articulates is his need to experience the whole of life, "the undivided sphere," in a spirit of reverence; his faith is in his capacity to pay attention to the world. Not for him is the restricted focus of one afflicted by habit: he wants to greet each day as if it were the first moment of Creation. Hence the enduring vitality of his poetry, which is filled with what Gerard Manley Hopkins called "the dearest freshness deep down things." Ghiselin's formal considerations—a tetrameter line, heavily enjambed, with enough variation to alert even careless readers to his rhythmic nuances; his clever play on cliches at the start of the second stanza; his subtle weaving together of disparate elements, ranging up and down from nightbirds to dew and desert to heaven, a journey in which human undertakings—"dream and empire"—are transcended;—all serve to create one of those "clear/ Sayings of the unsystematized." Brewster Ghiselin is a poet who celebrates language, even as he recognizes and revels in its limitations—those which make it possible for him to find his "untamed belief" gliding through the night sky.

by Christopher Merrill

Subjectivity

1.

Black bars expanding
        over an atomic-yellow ground—feelers retracted—
the monarch lay flat on the street
        and did not move at all
when I lifted it
        onto my spiral
notebook

        and did not move the whole length of the block
during which I held the purple laminated

cover still as
        possible—
my gaze
        vexing the edges of
the wings, ruffling the surface where it seemed
        light from another century
beat against those black bars—yellow, yellow, gorgeous, in-
                                                candescent—

        bells, chimes, flutes, strings—wind seized and blown
open—butter yellow, fever yellow,
        yellow of acid and flax,
lemon and chrome,
        madder, mikado, justice, canary—

yellow the singers exhale that rises, fanged, laughing,
        up through the architraves and out (slow) through the hard
                                                web
the rose-windows press
        onto the rising gaze,
yellow of cries forced through that mind's design,
        like a clean verdict,
like a structure of tenses and persons for the gusting

        heaven-yellow
minutes (so many flecks, spores,
        in the wide still beam
of sun)
        or the gaze's stringy grid of nerves
spreading out onto

whatever bright new world the eyes would seize upon—
pronged optic animal the incandescent *thing*
    must rise up to and spread into, and almost burn
                            its way
clear through
   to be.

     2.

   She sits on the straightback chair in the room.
A ray of sun is calling across the slatwood floor.
   I say *she* because my body is so still
in the folds of daylight
   through which the one beam slants.
I say *calling* because it lays itself down
   with a twang and a licking monosyllable

across the pine floor-boards—
   making a meaning like a wide sharp thought—
an unrobed thing we can see the inside of—
   less place than time—
less time than the shedding skin of time, the thought
                         of time,

the yellow swath it cuts
   on the continuum—
now to the continuum
   what she is to me,
a ceremonial form, an intransigent puissant corridor
                 nothing will intersect,

and yet nothing really
   —dust, a little heat . . .
She waits.
   Her leg extended, she waits for it—
foot, instep, calf—
   the I, the beam
of sun—
   the *now* and *now*—

it moving like a destiny across,
   neither lured-on nor pushed-forward,
without architecture,
   without
beginning,
   over the book lying in the dust,

over the cracked plank—down into the crack—across—

not animal,
    nothing that can be deduced-from or built-upon,
as warm with dust and yet
    not entered by the dust,
not *touched*—
    smearing everything with a small warm gaiety—

over the pillow-seam over the water glass—

    cracking and bending but not cracking or bending—

over the instep now, holding the foot—

    her waiting to feel the warmth then beginning
to feel it—
    the motion of it and the warmth of it not identical—
the one-way-motion of it, the slow sweep,
    approaching her as a fate approaches, inhuman but
                           resembling
feeling,

without deviation,
    turning each instant a notch deeper towards
the only forwards,
    but without beginning,
and never—not ever—
    not moving
forwards . . .

Meanwhile the knowledge of things lies round,
    over which the beam—
Meanwhile the transparent air
    through or into which the beam—
over the virtual and the material—
    over the world and over the world of the beholder—
glides:

    it does not change, crawler, but things are
changed—
    the mantle, the cotton-denim bunched at
                    the knees—

diamonds appearing on the tips of things then disappearing—
    each edge voluble with the plushnesses of silence—

now up to her folded arms—warm under the elbow—
almost a sad smell in the honeyed yellow—
    (the ridge of the collarbone) (the tuck of the neck)
till suddenly (as if by
    accident)

    she is inside—(ear, cheek)—the slice of time

now on the chin, now on
    the lips, making her rise up into me,
forcing me to close my eyes,
    the whole of the rest feeling broken off,

it all being my face, my being inside the beam of sun—

    and the sensation of how it falls unevenly,

    how the wholeness I felt in the shadow is lifted,
broken, this tip *lit*, this other *dark*—and stratified,
    analyzed, chosen-round, formed—

        3.

    Home I slid it gently
into the book,
    wings towards the center of the
page,
    the body denser and harder to press
flat,
    my mind hovering over it,
huge, ballooning, fluttering, yellow,
    and back and forth,
and searching for the heaviest book
    to lay upon
the specimen,
    to make it flat—

    as if it were still too plural, too
shade-giving, where the mind needs it
    so flat the light can't
round it, licking for crevices, im-
                        perfections,

even the wings still arced enough to bring
                        awake
    the secret blacknesses
of the page—

41

bits of shadow off the feelers, soft dry bits off
                                        the tiny
head—
    like a betrothal of the thing to the world—
a chattery, quivery moulting of

    the thing—body and wings—
so that each way I slide it the shadows slide—
    almost a green in their grey—
everything on the verge—
    the edge of the trunk furry—
the ever-so-slightly serrated rim of the wing—
    everywhere the soft grey exaggeration—
below, around—
    as if leaking from some *underneath*—

so that it is the *underneath* the mind wants to eliminate—
    the imitation? the interpretation?—
me carrying, through the bountiful morning-light, the dictionaries in—
    and the 2 inches of body and 5 inches of wing dripping with these
yellowish glances,
    these thin almost icy beams I can feel my open eyes release,
widening as they sweep down
    out of the retina

    to take the body in—
aerial, tunneling, wanting to be spent in what cannot
    feel them as they smear, coat,
wrap, diagram—

    from next door C stopping to bring the lilies in—
that butterfly's not dead, you know, she adds
    noticing,
cold mornings like these they're very still—*see* (gliding it onto
                                        the broad-leaved stem)
    put it in sun (walking back out),
the day like a tunnel she's in,
    the yellow thing at the end of her stalk and then,
placed on the lawn,
    the yellow thing, the specimen,
rising up of a sudden out of its envelope of glances—

a bit of fact in the light and then just light.

Linda Gregg

The Life of Literature

Very early in the morning at the edge of the capital
she is trying to get a ride. The huge machines
go past noisily, covering her with dust. She worries
about finding safe water or soda on the way.
Finally a man reaches down and helps her climb up
the wheel and over the side into the bed of the truck.
A young girl shifts to make room, then settles her
small brother's head in her lap. An old man turns
the blade of his machete away from them. When she
reaches Condega it is a quiet town. That night
she sits on a piece of cardboard in the garden
behind the house with the husband who used to live
with her. They look at the moon and talk
of poems in the book she lent him. The one
by Bāsho called *The Long Road into the Deep North.*

THIS POEM WAS WRITTEN FROM THE SIX MONTHS I LIVED IN NICARAGUA. WHILE THERE I WORKED
very hard to find a way to write poetry about the place without turning the place into literature—to get the place and the being there to the reader as itself rather than as a poem.

Donald Hall

Ox Cart Man

In October of the year,
he counts potatoes dug from the brown field,
counting the seed, counting
the cellar's portion out,
and bags the rest on the cart's floor.

He packs wool sheared in April, honey
in combs, linen, leather
tanned from deerhide,
and vinegar in a barrel
hooped by hand at the forge's fire.

He walks by his ox's head, ten days
to Portsmouth Market, and sells potatoes,
and the bag that carried potatoes,
flaxseed, birch brooms, maple sugar, goose
feathers, yarn.

When the cart is empty he sells the cart.
When the cart is sold he sells the ox,
harness and yoke, and walks
home, his pockets heavy
with the year's coin for salt and taxes,

and at home by fire's light in November cold
stitches new harness
for next year's ox in the barn,
and carves the yoke, and saws planks
building the cart again.

EVERY POEM SUGGESTS AN ARS POETICA. IN THE 1960S I WROTE SOMETHING CALLED "THE POEM," then late in the 1980s another called "This Poem." In between, I wrote "Ox Cart Man" in which (as I worked on it) I had no notice that I addressed the poet's purpose or task. I wrote an ars poetica anyhow. The ox-cart man's endless labor makes a cycle like a perennial plant's; writing the poem, I exulted in his annual rite of accumulation and dispersal. Not until I finished it, published it aloud and in print, did I become aware of a response that astonished me: Some people found it depressing: *all that work, and then he has to start over again.* (A faculty member, after a reading, said that it was like teaching composition; you drag through one term and then you have to start another.) Later, a friend compared the ox-cart man's story to a poet making a poem—and when I heard the notion, it rang true. For decades I have known that you must bring everything to a poem that you can possibly bring: Never hold anything back; spend everything at once—or you will never write a poem.

Only when you empty the well will the water return to the well.

Descendent

He came in where I lay all afternoon,
    Sleeping in unlikely sunlight,
And on his clipboard, made another check.
    Nod; check. The light shadowed him,
And he was still, and she in her chair, too,
    Until she crossed, about to shake.

She told him how to tell me I had cancer.
    "Tell her now." She knew, and whispered,
"She'll dream it, waking with the news in her body."
    I heard his checking sound, light
Across the pillows, sheets, and narrow wool,
    As pinged ice began to find the panes.

Check; nod; check; like archaic pelicans,
    Pecking their breasts for blood. The wind
Will cut the room in time for "Jeopardy."
    The doctor stood so far away.
Check; nod; check. He hadn't told me yet.
    His eyes like sheets of glass; the pupils

Putting their heads down. They don't know what to say.
    The TV doctor asked, "What is
The Pelican State?" And won a holiday
    From IVs arced above the gowns,
The waking patients, still as walls. The halls,
    Ammonia-lit. The carts of infants

Enter, leaving behind the mothers' rooms.
    She wouldn't want to see me cry,
So I told her she was crying. Did she
    Know it? Did she know how far
It spread? Nod; check the snow that skins
    Then swallows up the numb horizon.

Someone was supposed to wake, warm
    Again, bequeathing such forgiveness
To everyone. The sound resembled snow,
    Numb. I thought I'd like it: bodies
Washed and smothered, powdered blonde. Selected.
    "Sleep," he said. "Don't ask for more."

THE ARS POETICA EXISTS IN RELATION TO BOTH ART AND LIFE, THE WAY A CHILD VISITS PARENTS who share custody with ferocious bitterness. Resemblances are not acknowledged, or only secretly, or with a sense that what is shared betrays. These furtive contradictions initiate the writer. The poem becomes a poised assemblage, poised however briefly; and the ars poetica wears self-consciously its artifice, its metacognition. The writer, in some threshold state, turns her dream from a recurrence to a poem, formed; and then it presses—with the heft of its solidity imagined—against death's thigh.

Arse Poetica

You stand like a twin-headed bird,
one head open-mouthed in song,
the other stitched tight in sorrow.
An odd dance of *yin* and *yang*.

You simply cannot escape
your own original face.
The Greeks called this
excessive ego *hubris*,

consequence of the sin being
violence brought down
upon one's own head:
karma—pride's other twin.

Charmed, the storyteller
is always surprised
by the hard truths
of his own enchanting lies.

As one might, perhaps, come
to Literature—capital L—
only to find—what in hell?
Geoffrey Chaucer's bare red bum.

IN *MODERN MAN IN SEARCH OF A SOUL*, C.G. JUNG WRITES, "IT IS WELL KNOWN THAT GREAT minds have wrestled with the question whether it is the glorious sun that illuminates the worlds, or whether it is the human eye by virtue of its relation to the sun. Archaic man believes it to be the sun, and civilized man believes it is the eye—so far, at any rate, as he reflects at all and does not suffer from the disease of poets." The *dis-ease* of poets? To the eminent psychologist, perhaps, the disease of poets may be rooted in pathetic fallacy, in projecting false (human) attributes on a world. Civilized man (sic) must "strip nature of psychic attributes in order to dominate it; to see his world objectively he must take back all his archaic projections."

We must destroy, or at least alter, our perceptions of the "psyche" of old growth forests in order to perceive them as a "harvest." It is a troublesome problem, even when reduced to mere epistemology: our term *psyche* is derived from a Greek word for "breath" or animating principle of the world operating "as the soul animates human life." Is *psyche* therefore no more than a specious, grandiloquent pathetic fallacy? Gary Snyder asks whether trees should have legal standing.

Zen teaches that seer and seen are not two things. What the westerner calls *psyche* the Zen student comes to know as *mind* or *void*. The Taoist locates "mind" that binds *yin* and *yang* into a single thing. Is the world subjective or objective? And what is "reality"? The poet turns to literature for answers, the painter to imagery—whether abstracted or otherwise. The "line" of the poet, the "line" of the painter, the "line" of a good liar (read: mythologizer) all represent movement and stasis simultaneously; the "line" becomes a measure of our simultaneous wondering and knowing. But where does such a line begin and where does it end? Is my poem begun with an episode in Chaucer in the 14th century? Goode kinde Geoffrey's poetics is itself indebted to, among others, Catullus, who stole freely from Callimachus and other early Greeks, including Sappho (6th century b.c.e.), who in turn borrowed her musical "line" from the little stringed instrument called the *pektis* by Turks who invented it, borrowing *its* line. . . . The fundamental teaching of Zen is the idea of codependent origination.

A universe reflected in the pupil of a bird's eye, a bird, we might say, with "an attitude." In such a context, Chaucer's irreverent vertical grin becomes symbolic of cosmic laughter, the great wheel of the Dharma spinning silently on as we wonder in all our knowing.

∽₩₩₩∽

C. G. Hanzlicek

Osprey
for Dianne

Your father and mother were healthy then.
Maybe they weren't, though;
The body is a machine that seems well made,
But it is frail to the very cells,
And something may already have been at work
To take them.
They drove us through
Florida grazing land,
Filled with more cattle egrets than cattle,
To Lake Myakka.
A guide took us in a swamp boat
Over black water, espresso black
From tree bark tannin
Leeched out during floods.
The lake's reason for being
Seemed to be to give alligators a place
To perfect their boredom.
At the far end of the lake,
At the top of a dead tree,
Was a huge clot of sticks,
An osprey nest.
The guide had the motor idling,
And over its hum we heard a single,
Sharp cry of protest,
An agony I never want to hear again.
The guide wisely swung the boat around
And didn't hit the throttle
Until we were well away.
The swamp boat is an imperfect machine:
It does what it was built to do,

But with infernal noise.
The bicycle, on the other hand,
Is the most perfect machine ever built.
The heart of it, the chain,
Comes to us from no less a source
Than Leonardo's notebooks.
It does its work almost silently,
Just the whisper of links
Across the cogs,
And it gives back in well being
More than it takes in work.
Days ago, pedaling down a street
Lined with cork oaks,
I saw another perfect thing:
A skiff on a trailer.
It must have been put together
From plans of another century;
Instead of metal oarlocks,
There was a double set of wooden thole pins.
The varnish had been hand-rubbed
To a honeyed luster.
The top of the stern board
Was scrolled, and below the scrolling,
In gilt letters,
Was the boat's name: The Osprey.
I had just a few seconds' glimpse of it,
But I ached to have it
With the ache all
Finely made things cause in me.
If it were mine, though,
I could not bear to put that lovely
Artifact in water.
I'd toss out the living room furniture,
Put the boat in the center of the oriental rug,
Fill it with cushions and pillows,
And, aching for you,
Invite you in.
We could lie on our backs
And watch Arcturus
Track Ursa Major across the ceiling.
The rub and slosh of waves
Would wash away all thoughts
Of the frailty of mechanisms,
And we'd drift in the calm
Of a sea change.

Two statements have hovered like dark angels over my career as a poet. The first is Yeats' assertion that the only two things worthy of occupying the serious mind are sex and death. The poem "Osprey" touches upon both of these subjects. The other notion—and a far more disturbing one—comes from Czeslaw Milosz's introduction to the work of Tadeusz Rozewicz in an anthology of postwar Polish poetry. Milosz says that Rozewicz's own experiences in the war led him to hate art as an offense to human suffering. With these two angels whispering in my ear, my central ambition has simply been not to trivialize my art.

As regards technical matters, I have come to realize more and more over the years how much my father has shaped the way I look at craft. He was by trade a tool maker, and when he wasn't bent over one of his machines in the factory, his idea of relaxation was, as I once said in a poem, to "get lost in the softness of the wood" in his basement workshop. He was a happy man when he was doing the finishing sanding on some artifact he'd cut from black walnut. From him I learned to see beauty in utility and simplicity, which no doubt has a lot to do with why I've always gravitated toward a flat rather than a decorative voice.

In "Osprey" I call the bicycle the most perfect machine ever built; it is such a beautiful mechanism because it does an enormous amount of work quietly and efficiently. I would someday like to write a poem that I could look upon the way I look at a Merlin titanium frame bike equipped with Campagnolo Record components, something that is beautiful because attention has been paid to details, because it shifts smoothly, because it gives more than it takes, because it enhances one's own internal power instead of relying on something external for drive.

Spring Drawing 2

A man says *lilacs against white houses, two sparrows, one streaked in a thinning birch*, and can't find his way to a sentence.

In order to be respectable, Thorstein Veblen said, desperate in Palo Alto, a thing must be wasteful, i.e., "a selective adaptation of forms to the end of conspicuous waste."

So we try to throw nothing away, as Keith, making dinner for us as his grandmother had done in Jamaica, left nothing; the kitchen was as clean at the end as when he started; even the shrimp shells and carrot fronds were part of the process,

and he said, when we tried to admire him, "Listen, I should send you into the chickenyard to look for a rusty nail to add to the soup for iron."

The first temptation of Sakyamuni was desire, but he saw that it led to fulfillment and then to desire, so that one was easy.

Because I have pruned it badly in successive years, the climbing rose has sent out, among the pale pink floribunda, a few wild white roses from the rootstalk.

Suppose, before they said *silver* or *moonlight* or *wet grass*, each poet had to agree to be responsible for the innocence of all the suffering on earth,

because they learned in arithmetic, during the long school days, that if there was anything left over,

you had to carry it. The wild rose looks weightless, the floribunda are heavy with the richness and sadness of Europe

as they imitate the dying, petal by petal, of the people who bred them.

You hear pain singing in the nerves of things; it is not a song.

The gazelle's head turned; three jackals are eating his entrails and he is watching.

I DON'T THINK I'VE EVER WRITTEN A POEM THAT SEEMED TO ME ENTIRELY SATISFACTORY AS AN ars poetica. But then I don't think I've ever written a poem that seemed to me entirely satisfactory. I remember someone saying that lyric poetry is "partial" in both senses of the word. The poem finds itself in what one is partial to, and every saying seems part of the story, only part of the world, or of the representation of one's experience of it. There is an early poem of mine called "Measure" that speaks with gratitude, I guess, of one experience I've had of the source of poems. It begins:

> Recurrences.
> Coppery light hesitates
> again in the small-leaved
>
> Japanese plum. Summer
> and sunset, the peace
> of the writing desk
>
> and the habitual peace
> of writing, these things
> form an order I only
>
> belong to in the idleness
> of attention . . .

I think now that the background of this poem, the violent years of the Vietnam War, isn't sufficiently implicit in it. This opposition between the open spirit of attention and the active violence of the world was something I experienced very strongly when I was beginning to write. It was a feeling close, I suppose, to Wordsworth's "wise passivity" but it didn't seem to me at the time a literary idea. It was something I experienced intensely and found echoed in the Japanese and Chinese poems I had been reading at that time which seemed to me not partial, to open themselves with such clarity of mind and such freedom from prehensile, conceptual imposition on what was seen that they really did make an entire reality. "Measure" was, I suppose, a poem of that wish but it certainly doesn't achieve the condition it wishes toward.

I've heard that when Monet embarked on the waterlily paintings, he had them in mind as a response to the dead in the trenches of the first World War. Knowing that intention, I thought, would change the paintings when I looked at them again, might very well make their great beauty seem at some level unforgivable, but it doesn't. I remember walking into the Monet gallery one Sunday morning in—where—the Orangerie or the Jeu de Paume and being surrounded by those huge tranquil canvases and feeling that, if they were a response to heaped corpses, the pain of families that would be numbered by years and habits, the stupidity and brutality of a particular idea of civilization embodied in an officer corps full of ambition acquired at class-ridden military academies, in war rooms full of politicians, then there was something brutal and triumphantly defiant in the paintings.

Later I would think that the difference between my old thought of the rebellious counter-idea of peacefulness in art and this huge thing Monet had done had to do with the idea of making, not receiving order or peace from the natural world. That art of great beauty only got made if it swallowed great gobbets of the pain and suffering and senselessness of the world whole and survived it in the act of making. Years of studying Milosz, as I worked on getting his poems into English, sharpened this sense for me, Milosz who sometimes seemed to think that any praise of this world colluded with the unspeakable suffering of every living creature, and I suppose it is these thoughts which lie behind "Spring Drawings 1 and 2" from *Human Wishes*. Parts, I suppose, of an ongoing ambivalence, inside which, I suppose, I try to believe that the gesture of art can matter. At least the supreme examples seem to say so.

Juan Filipe Herrera

El Secreto de mis Brazos	The Secret of My Arms
El secreto de mis brazos	The secret of my arms
un oro de la tiniebla	a bit of gold in the dimness
el rumbo de mi sangre	the course of my blood
un ala del mar	a wing from the sea
el tríangulo de mis caminos	the triangle of my roads
una estrella de tu boca	a star of your mouth
la blusa de mi guitarra	the blouse of my guitar
una piedra de gaviotas	a stone of gulls
el dibujo de mi garganta	the sketch of my throat
un aceite de tus ojos	an oil of your eyes
la flama de mi frente	the flame of my forehead
un lunar de tu llanto	a beauty mark of your tears
la soledad de mis manos	the solitude of my hands
el secreto de mis brazos	the secret of my arms

Translated by Stephen Kessler and Sesshu Foster

Her Name Is *Señorita Solitary Ash*: On Writing

FEVER, VELOCITY, OPEN TOMBS—A SELF-CIRCUS BLOWN OUT AND PERFORMED BY THE VISCERA, the fancy melting moment that surrounds me: this is my act of starting up the words, the spillage on paper, this ars poetica. A continuous Thalo Red talk, a breakage into texture, soul-snap and a document somewhere in-between the ache and the numbness and the joy that peers through me. Open tombs are best; to be able to crack into my depths, into my swollen basement and then excavate under these sites a bit more, find the bones, the fuzzy faces, moth wings and the long red tooth of my *monstrous*. It takes fever, hot flashes in the open throat. And then, of course, Ms. Fellini walks in, paints my nose ochre yellow and pulls my màscara. This is what happens inside and a little under my eyes, up my sleeves. Craft isn't necessary; anyone who talks craft post-1964 is dead, dead. Remember 1964? Year of Color and New Colonies for the Carousel of the US of A? Maxim: Don't talk craft if it is killing you. King Craft is my enemy, first-cousin to the Academy and its blue-vested emissaries of High Apprenticeship and Empire Indulgence. Let's throw the head back twice like in the new Latino Dance craze initiated by Victor Hernandez-Cruz and Margarita Luna Robles; and then shoo-bop into the scene. The scene, even if Ms. Fellini presides at the podium, the scene is marvelous, unkempt, like You & Me; remember them too. So, when You & Me head out the door and face the jagged slate, we listen up to the tik-tok, up high, up by the compassionate mug of the political organ-man, the Pres in this case, yes—in most cases a man. Here comes the fever, down my wavy breast-bone. So, I talk it fast, the way I sees it, inside-outside and of course (my favorite) the in-between game. Keep the language unknown, keep it mixing, do a mix-out and mix-in, heaven and hell or hell #1 and hell #5. If you meet old lovers, greet them and they will stay for a Café Olé. *¿Como esta?* You & Me will sing this. And Señorita Solitary Ash will call-back wisely, guffaw and scratch. Picasso will be there too, in his favorite striped beach wear, maybe with Maria Felix and Robin Williams throwing green popcorn at the tiny bulls. All this belongs to no one. All this cannot be printed; yeah, this is Life in the Circus. How are You & Me going to publish Emmet Kelly's love affair with Caligula? Queen Somalia's belly dance with the Count Georgio Bush. Think of the proper costumes for the Sarajevo Trapeze. For the Bosnia Human Cannonball. Love is in the air; that's why gas masks are given at the ticket booth. No one knows where You & Me are headed. You are wearing your almost-lost James Dean look-alike melancholy and Me is wearing the aloof Denim every Zincanteco Indian trucker hauling artificial flowers from Mexico City to Tuxtla Gutierrez desires & admires as his sacred cargo; a kiss from UZ. Where is my biography? Forgot it, hated it. Where is my autobiography? Can't say it when I am driving the auto, gets caught in the neck-axle; so I burn it and tease the flame. Señorita Solitary Ash is here, gives me good advice.

Emily Hiestand

Chain of Species

The top carnivores are the obvious ones,
but in the subtle chain, the ribbed mussel
of the marshes invites admiration:

When marsh grass is swept to sea
to decompose and fill the water
with slurries of phosphorus bits,

the humble mussel begins to work.
Three days pass. Phosphorus particles
are filtered, firmly placed in a marl,

to be by mud-feeders released,
to grasses and planktons, who spoonfeed
the fishes whose droppings are taken

by grasses as delicacies, moving them
to sweep again to the muscular sea:
a cycle familiar to us from *Golden Books*,

whose pictures neglect to say
that it all takes place in a rigorous tide,
rocking the bi-valves in their shells.

MUSSELS HAVE VERY LITTLE TO SAY ABOUT THEIR LABORS.

Brenda Hillman

Little Furnace

—Once more the poem woke me up,
the dark poem. I was ready for it;
he was sleeping,

and across the cabin, the small furnace
lit and re-lit itself—the flame a yellow
    "tongue" again, the metal benignly
hard again;

and a thousand insects outside called
    and made me nothing;
moonlight streamed inside as if it had been . . .

I looked around, I thought of the lower wisdom,
spirit held by matter:
    Mary, white as a sand dollar,

and Christ, his sticky halo tilted—
    oh, to get behind it!
The world had been created to comprehend itself

as matter: table, the torn
veils of spiders . . . Even consciousness—
missing my love—

was matter, the metal box of a furnace.
As the obligated flame, so burned my life . . .

What is the meaning of this suffering I asked
and the voice—not Christ but between us—said
you are the meaning.

No, no, I replied, That
is the shape, what is the meaning.
You are the meaning, it said—

ONE IDEA I HAD FOR A WHILE WAS THAT IT IS POSSIBLE TO "SUM UP" A CONDITION WHEN writing of an event. I had been thinking, because I'm involved with gnostic ideas of inner light, that a condition could be *inside* a thing.

It also seemed good to write poems you might want to memorize. This involves staying satisfied.

The title "Little Furnace" is something of a lie; the object in question is a small water heater in my lover's house, not a furnace. I wasn't sure whether I approved of matter by that point or not. As to the thematic content: I have tried many times to write about this: the sense of being *stuck* being here, and of being pleased that something is in the process of forgiving this stuckness. The idea that meaning might yield itself from resistance—I don't know why I find this so appealing, but it is one thing I believe when I lie awake in the night. It seems acceptable to be alive with this possibility.

Perhaps it's important to write poems that do not betray us—or get it wrong—but that's a lot of responsibility to put on a poem. I'm not sure about an ars poetica but I would think this poem might serve as a representative.

Edward Hirsch

Sortes Virgilianae
(The Fortuneteller's Words to the Poet)

"I don't understand, I can scarcely see
In the faulty light, but I think he is standing
On a platform somewhere below the ground.

He is a shadow lost amid shadows, a wave
On the watery stairs, a shade testing
The fetid air and touching the fog.

I see him taking a tentative step forward
And then another and another until the dark
Stumbles and welcomes him into its grasp.

Disconsolate being, a train shudders
In the distance overhead, and I remember
A wind whirling and spitting him out,

Steel doors opening and then clanging shut,
A branch glowing on the floor beneath the seat—
Untouched, forgotten. What does this mean?

The way downward is easy from Avernus.
Black Dis's door stands open night and day.
But to retrace your steps to heaven's air,

There is the trouble, there is the hard task.
And now he is wandering through a labyrinth
Of dead-end corridors and empty tunnels,

Broken mirrors and smudged signs pointing
Nowhere, voices echoing like footsteps
In the iron hallways. Listen to me:

If you want to become more than a shadow
Among shadows, you must carry back the memory
Of your father disintegrating in your arms,

You must bring words that will console others,
You must believe in stairs leading upward
To summer's resplendent, celestial blues."

IN "SORTES VIRGILIANAE" A FORTUNETELLER, A DIVINER OF MYSTERIES, EXPLAINS TO A POET, A maker, what he must do to fulfill his true vocation. The title refers to the ancient practice of fortunetelling by choosing at random a passage from Virgil's poetry. This appealing, somewhat degraded game of Virgilian fates combines chance and necessity, luck, explication, and revelation.

What the fortuneteller sees—the substance of the poem—is a solitary wanderer, an Aeneas-like figure, trying to make his way through the dark underworld. The passage chosen is one of the most poignant in *The Aeneid*, beloved by Freud and Eliot alike. The italicized lines, whereby the Sibyl speaks to Aeneas at the mouth of the cave, are from

Book VI, "The World Below" (lines 129-132). I rely on Robert Fitzgerald's splendid translation, though I have modified the crucial last phrase.

The final six lines encapsulate an oblique ars poetica. The poet is specifically charged to carry the past into the future, to articulate and inscribe what would otherwise be lost or forgotten. The keeper of language gives voice to the Other. Making poetry is taken as psychological descent, a way into the labyrinth, but it also becomes a struggle upward, a path out. What is sought is a poetry of suffering and of joy that gives body to shadows.

Jane Hirshfield

Justice without Passion

My neighbor's son, learning piano,
moves his fingers through the passages
a single note at a time, each lasting an equal interval,
each of them loud, distinct,
deliberate as a camel's walk through sand.
For him now, all is dispassion, a simple putting in place;
and so, giving equal weight to each mark in his folded-back book,
bending his head towards the difficult task,
he is like a soldier or a saint: blank-faced, and given wholly
to an obedience he does not need to understand.
He is even-handed, I think to myself,
and so, just. But in what we think of as music
there is no justice, nor in the evasive beauty of this boy,
glimpsed through his window across the lawn,
nor in what he will become, years from now, whatever he will become.
For now though, it is the same to him:
right note or wrong, he plays only for playing's sake
through the late afternoon, through stumbling and error,
through children's songs, Brahms, long-rehearsed, steady progressions
as he learns the ancient laws—that human action is judgement,
each note struggling with the rest.
That justice lacking passion fails, betrays.

I DIDN'T THINK OF THIS POEM AS AN ARS POETICA UNTIL SOMEONE WHO WAS TEACHING IT THAT way mentioned it to me, but as soon as I heard it, I immediately recognized that was right. Not that I don't still think the poem is also about what it appears to be about—a boy studying piano; a wider view of what might constitute true justice than our usual conception of a blindfolded figure holding a scale—but the eye that looks outward also, inevitably and always, sees inward at the same time.

Describing as accurately, honestly, and completely as we can the world as it appears to us, we simultaneously discover the self: its lineaments of desire, its body, its morals, its thoughts. The poem's statement is that for any conception of human truth to *be* accurate, honest, or complete, it needs to contain the full range of human experience and feeling—the bruised heart as well as the clear mind, the passionate body as well as the skills of right technique, the knowledge that fate is not necessarily fair, that we do not control our lives; and that still the road is found in the persistent walking of it, in the dogged following of experience lived through. Letting all this come into us, there begins to be the possibility of making by means of the instruments of our words and tongues and histories, and out of the deep rhythms of heart, body, and mind, a genuine music.

Garrett Hongo

Stay with Me

At six o'clock, most people
already sitting down to dinner
and the Evening News, Gloria's
still on the bus, crying
in a back seat, her face
bathed in soft blue light
from the fluorescent lamps.
She leans her head down
close to her knees, tugs
at the cowl of her raincoat
so it covers her eyes, tries
to mask her face and stifle
the sobbing so the young black
in the seat across the aisle
won't notice her above the
disco music pouring from
his radio and filling the bus.
He does anyway, and, curious,
bends towards her, placing a hand
on her shoulder, gently,
as if consoling a child
after the first disappointment,
asking, "Is it cool, baby?"

She nods, and, reassured,
he starts back to his seat,
but she stops him, sliding
her hand over his, wanting
to stroke it, tapping it instead,
rhythmically, as if his hand
were a baby's back and she
its mother, singing and rocking
it softly to sleep. The black
wishes he could jerk his hand

away, say something hip to save
himself from all that's not
his business, something like
"Get back, Mama! You a fool!"
but he can't because Gloria's
just tucked her chin over
both their hands, still resting
on her shoulder, clasped them
on the ridge of her jaw the way
a violinist would hold a violin.

He can feel the loose skin
around her neck, the hard bone
of her jaw, the pulse
in her throat thudding against
his knuckles, and still he wants
to pull away, but hesitates,
stammers, asks again,
"Hey . . . Is it okay?"

He feels something hot
hit his arm, and, too late
to be startled now, sighs
and gives in, turning his
hand over, lifting it, clasping
hers, letting her bring it
to her cheek, white and slick
with tears, stroking her face
with the back of his hand,
rubbing the hollow of her cheek
against his fist, and she,
speaking finally, "Stay with me
a little while. Till your stop?
Just stay with me," as her face
blooms and his shines
in the blue fluorescent light.

ALL MY TEENAGE LIFE, COMING UP STUPID AND TOUGH IN THE STRANGE, ALIEN WORLD OF
South Central Los Angeles, I wanted for what was given easily to me as a child in Hawaii.
The city simply didn't have it.

I wanted *mercy*. I wanted the universe to bend down and kiss its own creation, like a
parent does to a child just after it's born, as if a pure tenderness were the expression of the
world for itself. I wanted to believe that what was not given, *could* be given, that were a
man or a woman to cry out for solace, that the world, for all of its steel plants and tire fac-
tories, for all of its liquor stores and razor wire, for all of its buses that belched carcino-
genic poisons and people who passed you by on the freeway who cursed you with their
eyes; for all of that, I wanted to believe the heavens would still lay its soft wings of blessing
upon you if you cried out in need. It was *aloha*—the breath of love upon your face.

Richard Hugo

The House on 15th S.W.

Cruelty and rain could be expected.
Any season. The talk was often German
and we cried at the death of strangers.
Potatoes mattered and neighbors who came
to marvel at our garden. I never helped
with the planting. I hid in woods these houses
built on either side replaced. Ponds
duplicated sky. I watched my face
play out dreams of going north with clouds.

North surely was soft. North was death
and women and the women soft. The tongue
there was American and kind. Acres of women
would applaud me as I danced, and acres
of graves would dance when sun announced
another cloud was dead. No grating scream
to meals or gratuitous beatings,
no crying, raging fists against closed doors,
twisted years I knew were coming at me,
hours alone in bars with honest mirrors,
being fun with strangers, being liked
so much the chance of jail was weak
from laughter, and my certainty of failure
mined by a tyrant for its pale perverted ore.

My pride in a few poems, my shame
of a wasted life, no wife, no children,
cancel out. I'm neutral as this house,
not caring to go in. Light would be soft
and full, not harsh and dim remembered.
The children, if there are children inside,
would be normal, clean, not at all
the soiled freaks I had counted on.

I MIGHT HAVE CHOSEN "DEGREES OF GRAY IN PHILIPSBURG" FOR THIS ANTHOLOGY, AND I THINK
a lot of people who know and love Richard Hugo's poems well might have, too. The
poem is set in a stark, eroded Montana town. "Our triggering subjects," Hugo wrote, "like
our worlds, come from obsessions we must submit to, whatever the social cost." The bat-
tle between those obsessions and the consolations they drive us to seek is central to the
poem. Like so many of Hugo's poems, this one is a useful parody of the Western. A
stranger, not tall and not violent, comes into town, and nothing is changed; the gunfight
between the obsessions and consolations doesn't happen.

   The last two stanzas of the poem I didn't pick go like this:

> Isn't this your life? That ancient kiss
> still burning out your eyes? Isn't this defeat
> so accurate, the church bell simply seems
> a pure announcement: ring and no one comes?
> Don't empty houses ring? Are magnesium

and scorn sufficient to support a town,
not just Philipsburg, but towns
of towering blondes, good jazz and booze
the world will never let you have
until the town you came from dies inside?

Say no to yourself. The old man, twenty
when the jail was built, still laughs
although his lips collapse. Someday soon,
he says, I'll go to sleep and not wake up.
You tell him no. You're talking to yourself.
The car that brought you here still runs.
The money you buy lunch with,
no matter where it's mined, is silver
and the girl who serves you food
is slender and her red hair lights the wall.

Philipsburg, it seems, peaked during the silver boom. The speaker, too, is taunted by past glories: "The last good kiss/you had was years ago."

The turn in the poem, at the end of the third stanza (and first of the two I quote above), is a peculiar moment. For what are those "towns/of towering blondes, good jazz and booze" but the Heaven of Hugh Hefner, what "the world will never let you have/until the town you came from dies inside?" Those lines sound like an analyst speaking, or a good analysand skillfully prodded. They are really an answer to a question the poem doesn't ask, at least explicitly: Why do these run-down towns remind me of why I think so badly of myself?

Then the character and poem alike say no to despair, count small blessings and get ready to drive off into the sunset.

It's the combination of how directly the poem faces its desperations and its final jauntiness that make us love the poem: it has the same emotional bravery his friends loved in Hugo.

But it isn't the poem in which the confrontation gets made for which this and Hugo's other Montana poems are obsessive rehearsals. That poem is "The House on 15th St. S.W."

The location is White Center, a neighborhood of working-class immigrants in West Seattle where Hugo was raised by stern and emotionally crippled grandparents, and where powerful and steady blows were dealt to the boy's self-love.

No towering blondes here. The women are equally figures of fantasy, specifically associated with cold, North and death. Here speech is assimilated, and not harsh. It's the heaven of WASPs, where families never raise their voices, and surely seemed as impossible to a boy as the fraternity party heaven in the Philipsburg poem did to the man that boy became.

Instead there were the terrors, the "twisted years I knew were coming at me," and the consolations, the "hours alone in bars with honest mirrors,/ being fun with strangers."

Hugo drives into the Montana towns, but at the house in which he grew up, "neutral. . . , not caring to go in," he performs a small ceremony and goes away. Or rather he performs a small ceremony *by* going away.

There is an Ambrose Bierce story in which a man has a recurring dream. He is traveling on a road he uses every day of his waking life, and in the dream he notices a slight break in the woods alongside his route. He turns his buggy into it, and it's a driveway. It leads to a beautiful house. He feels almost hypnotized, fully compelled. He goes to the door and knocks. An old crone answers. "Who owns the house?" he asks. "I'll pay any sum to own and live in this house."

"I'm sorry," says the crone, as she shuts the door slowly. "I can't sell it. It's haunted." And there the dream ends.

One day in waking life he is traveling along the road and sees the slight break in the woods. He turns in and there it is at the end of the driveway, his dream house. He goes to the door. The crone answers. They both know their lines.

". . . I can't sell it. It's haunted." Except this is waking life, and the dream doesn't end here.

60

"Haunted?" he says. "By whom?"

"By you," replies the crone, and closes the door, and Bierce closes his story.

By walking away, Hugo unhaunts the house. The children inside, if there are children inside, are freed from being soiled freaks for no better reason than to keep fresh the metaphors of Hugo's childhood pain. He gives up his power over the house, and in return it ceases to be a portable stage setting for pain and resumes its life as a house. It's an even ("neutral") trade. The two sides "cancel out," like pride in a few poems and shame of a wasted life. You trade with what you've got.

This was the tough poem to write, and it made possible the last love poems and the cackling, antic poems written on the Isle of Skye. For now women were women rather than symbols, and the world was the world.

That's not an angel you're wrestling, it turns out. It's you. The great mature ars poetica poem for Hugo was the one in which he first called out clearly for a truce, and unhanded himself.

by William Matthews

Lynda Hull

Cubism, Barcelona

So easily you fall to sleep, the room a cage of rain,
the wallpaper's pinstripe floral another rift
between us, this commerce of silences and mysteries
called marriage, but that's not what this is about.

It's this wet balcony, filigreed, this rusty fan of spikes
the pensione's installed against thieves and this weather—

needling rain that diminuendoes into vapor, fog
dragging its cat's belly above the yellow spikes
of leaves, the hungry map the hustlers make stitching through
the carnival crowd below, and I'm thinking of Picasso's

early work—an exhibit of childhood notebooks, a *Poetics'*
margins twisting with doves and bulls and harlequins. Your face,

our friends', the sullen milling Spaniards, repeated canvases
of faces dismantled, fractured so as to contain
the planar flux of human expression—boredom to lust
and fear, then rapture and beyond. He was powerless,

wasn't he, before all that white space? I mean he had to
fill it in, and I can fill in the blank space of this room

between you and me, between me and the raucous promenade,
with all the rooms and galleries I've known, now so wantonly
painting themselves across this room, this night, the way
I extend my hand and the paseo, foreign beyond my fingertips,

dissolves to a familiar catastrophe of facades, the angles
of walls and ceilings opening all the way to the waterfront

where the standard naked lightbulb offers its crude flower
of electricity to blue the dark abundant hair a woman
I could have been is brushing, a torn shade rolled up to see
the bird vendor's cat upon his shoulder or, at some other stage

in their pursuit, the same French sailor I see drunkenly
courting the queen dolled up in bedsheet and motorcycle chain,

some drag diva strung out on something I can't name, something
kicking this vicious twin inside who longs to walk
where guidebooks say not to, who longs to follow beyond all
common sense, that childhood love of terror propelling us

through funhouses and arcades, mother of strange beauty and faith.
But it's only chill rain that gathers in my palm, the empty

terra-cotta pots flanking the balcony. Rain and the ache
in my hands today, those off-tilt Gaudis queasily spelling
the tilt from port to port any life describes: Boston's damp cold
and we're stuffing rags again in broken windows, that condemned

brownstone on harshly passionate—Mr. Lowell—Marlborough Street
where our feet skimmed, polished black across the floor,

damp, the tattered hems of trousers. Simply trying like always
to con our way to some new dimension. And weren't we glamorous?
Oh, calendar pages riffling in the artificial wind
of some offscreen fan, a way to show life passing, the blurred

collage of images we collect to show everything and nothing
has changed. But I want to talk about the swans of Barcelona

this afternoon in the monastery pool, battered palms
and small bitter oranges smashed against pavement stones.
And those swans, luxurious and shrill by turns. It's not swans
that arrest me now—only this sailor staggering on the paseo

fisting the air between him and the queen, shouting *je sens, je sens,*
but he isn't able to say what he feels any more than I understand

how it is that perspective breaks down, that the buried life
wants out on sleepless nights amidst these coils of citizens,
a carnival dragon snaking, sodden, through the trees above them.
I know. I know, there's got to be more than people ruthlessly

hurricaned from port to port. I know tomorrow is a prayer
that means hope, that now you breathe softly, sleeping face

rent by sooted shadows the thief's grille throws while you're
turned into whatever dream you've made of these curious days
filled with cockatoos and swans, the endless rain.
Things get pretty extreme, then tomorrow little blades

of grass will run from silver into green
down the esplanade where a waiter places

ashtrays on the corners of tablecloths
to keep them firmly anchored.
The drag queen will be hustling, down on her knees
in the subway, a few exotic feathers twisting in the wind.

But it won't be me, Jack. It won't be me.

THIS POEM AND ANOTHER ONE IN *STAR LEDGER* CALLED "CARNIVAL" ORIGINALLY STARTED AS A
single letter to a friend written after I'd spent some time in Barcelona, that marvelous hal-
lucinatory port city that was the anarchist center of Spain during the Civil War. Picasso
did much of his early pre-Paris work there and a museum dedicated to his youthful work
has a collection of his schoolbooks, including a copy of Aristotle's *Poetics.* The books were
filled compulsively with sketches—all the leitmotifs he'd explore throughout his career
were there as marginalia—bulls, harlequins, doves. That and the city, various chance
encounters I had there, acted on me along with the sense of being strange to yourself trav-
el can cause. I like this poem because it does what I want my work to do, a kind of formal
anarchy, "luxurious and shrill by turns" with language that rollercoasters from elegance to
street slang. The notion of Cubism let me explore "the planar flux" not only of "human
expression" but of the self, of memory, constructs that seem permeable to me, multiple.

T. R. Hummer

Ohio Abstract: Hart Crane

Factory aether thickens over the milky lake at sunrise,
Imperially, like smoke from the last cigar of the Czar.
Bruised faces of stevedores clarify along the docks
As if a metaphysical fluoroscope were touching them

With infiltrating radiation—on the other side, the skeletal
Shape of a crane appears against white buildings.
The tannery whistle agitates. This is inescapably Cleveland.
It is morning now, and the bridge remains the bridge.

Down by the stockyard fence, a man in a pea-coat staggers.
He was up all night drinking dago red. A sailor let him
Suck his dick, then blackmailed him for ten dollars.
Now he'll work sixteen hours in a warehouse shifting

Crates of chocolate hearts stamped out for the glorious balls
Of a second-rate midwestern Gilded Age. It isn't the money
That worries him, the thirty cents an hour. It isn't top-hats
Or new puce gloves. He can't forget the synaesthesia,

The luminous foretaste of sweat, those syncopated mystical chimes
In the background of his fumbling at the fly-buttons,
The disciplined, improvised slant-rhyme of *denim* and *tongue*.
Blinding, the incense of horseshit in the gutter.

He chokes on the ecstatic rumble of the fourth dimension's junk-carts.
Lonely and stupid and sad, the *Don't you love me?* of the barges.
And what are those great water-birds writing down there by the garbage?
In this illusion of space, nothing could ever have existed.

Wrong sex. Wrong sense. Wrong city. Wrong bridge. Wrong life.
But who needs another elegy? No one ever dies here either.
It just goes on and on, gold foil on an assembly line, two tons
Of hearts for New York City. *Metaphor*, riffs the streetcar,

Is *bear over* in the literal Greek. But who says *what*
Or *how heavy?* Blackjack. Crowbar. Hammer. A man
Coldcocked by the shadow of a telephone pole. Think of all they tell you
The soul holds up in the men's room of the Tower of Light.

Maybe nothing ever meant more on earth than what it weighs.

Inside the Avalanche

1. IN THE FOREWORD OF *THE FACT OF A DOORFRAME: POEMS SELECTED AND NEW, 1950-1984*, Adrienne Rich raises, with typical wisdom and incisiveness, a crucial issue about the relationship between craft and the particular consciousness of any poet:

> One task for the nineteen- or twenty-year-old
> poet who wrote the earliest poems here was to
> learn that she was neither unique nor
> universal, but a person in history. . . . The
> learning of poetic craft was much easier than
> knowing what to do with it—with the powers,
> temptations, privileges, potential
> deceptions, and two-edged weapons of
> language.

The complexities of this position—exemplified so fully in the body of Rich's work—I take as fundamental. Who writes my poems? Do they represent what I believe they represent—in either the aesthetic or the political meaning of representation?

2. A RECENT REREADING OF *VOYAGER*, JOHN UNTERECKER'S BIOGRAPHY OF HART CRANE, underscored the knot of unanswerable questions that must attend any meditation on biography and the art of poetry. How can one even begin to understand with any precision the connections between the details of Hart Crane's life—from the most profound to the most mundane—and his poetry? Is it profitable to think, when we read *The Bridge*, of Crane's Cleveland adolescence, of his homosexuality, of his love of dancing, of his peculiar autodidact's sense of literature and of the history of culture, of his alcoholism, of his longing for visionary experience, of his father's career as a manufacturer of luxury candies (he invented Lifesavers and sold the proletariat idea cheap), of his curious and dreary suicide? No, I want to say: the poetry is not informed by these particulars or any of a million others reported in Unterecker's massive book—any more than our understanding of Crane's poems depends on facts that have never and will never come to light, for how could that be? But at the same time there obviously is a connection between every fact of Crane's life—whether known to us or unknown forever—and his poems. Otherwise, there is no reason for Crane's poems to have been written by Crane; they might as well have been written by you or by me.

3. A POET THINKS THESE THOUGHTS WITH A CERTAIN DESPERATION. HOW, EXACTLY, ARE THE details of my own life connected to the poems I write? What does it mean to be "neither unique nor universal?" Why are my poems, for better or worse, written by me and not by you or by Hart Crane?

4. POETRY, I THINK, IS NO ONE THING; IT IS RATHER, AS FOUCAULT SAYS OF ANY GENEALOGY, "an unstable assemblage of faults, fissures, and heterogeneous layers that threaten the inheritor from within or underneath." Confronting the body of work of any poet—confronting poetry *per se*—it is as if we were faced by a vast avalanche held back, perhaps, by a system of cables and pulleys barely adequate to the task of impeding its forward course even momentarily. Thinking of that agglomerate as a unity, we say to ourselves, "Look: there is a *cliff*."

No matter how monolithic it may appear to any particular observer, poetry is in fact constantly and forever in a state of dismemberment. Therefore, the dismemberment of poetry is no source of concern except as a condition to be described and studied—and admired. The self, too, is an avalanche, not a unity; but it insists on experiencing its own collapse as a forward motion into the world: it insists on describing itself *to* itself as *a* self. The only dismemberment that can matter—as a source of fear and exaltation—is the dismemberment of individual poets. The dismemberment matters because it is the only one that can lead to a resurrection. This is one of the reasons why the "tragic" life of such a poet as Hart Crane is of such interest to us: we imagine, arguably wrongly, that we see in it with particular clarity the torque and strain of living inside the avalanche.

5. THERE ARE GOOD REASONS FOR OUR PREOCCUPATION WITH SUCH MATTERS—EVEN BEYOND the pleasures of gossip. For example, one of the most mysterious moments in the history of poetry, the genealogy of the art, is the moment when Walt Whitman became Walt Whitman. That is, from the point of view of criticism and biography, the moment when Whitman became the man capable of writing *Leaves of Grass*. The mistake is to conceive of such a thing as taking place all in a moment. The resurrection of Christ required three narrative days—and who knows how much time was required for Dionysus to pull himself together?

The world dismembers poets; only poetry dismembers poetry. (This will cease to be the case when the world elects to dismember humanity.)

6. "OHIO ABSTRACT: HART CRANE" IS NOT A POEM BASED IN ANY RIGOROUS WAY ON THE "facts" of the life of Hart Crane; neither is it autobiographical in any way I am able to recognize. Its genesis lies somewhere midway in my reading of Unterecker and simultaneously of Crane's poems; it also lies in my own struggle to discover the political and personal consequences of beauty, both philosophically and as I have registered its irradiation through the untrustworthy geiger counter of my own flesh and nerves. Czeslaw Milosz's unsettling poem "*Ars Poetica?*" comes as close as anything I know to describing the ambiguous set of relations out of which such poems come:

> The purpose of poetry is to remind us
> how difficult it is to remain just one person,
> for our house is open, there are no keys in the doors,
> and invisible guests come in and out at will.

7. IT IS POSSIBLE TO REGARD THE PECULIAR REFRACTION CONNECTING POETRY AND THE DETAILS of a poet's life—as if they were two separate categories—as a productive synaesthesia. It is possible to describe the process that bears over the weight of history into the shape of a given poem as the highest form of metaphorical activity. It is possible to maintain, without being in the least mystical or psychologically reductive, that Crane's poems are not only Crane's poems, that mine or yours are not only mine or yours.

The world dismembers poets—but poetry, and poets, are part of the world. Unique? Universal? The white space between *ars* and *poetica* contains multitudes.

Mark Irwin

On Language

By a green pond he sits
and watches two swans move
like slow patches of ice
as the pewtery sun
gives way to a hesitant
rain. The page

he reads is
O.K., but its taste
does not spread into his mind
as do the vodka,
cigarette, and scarlet crests
of oaks

until he touches it
to the hot red
ash, and sees
how flames doused
by the drying rain
give what slow gold
that poem cannot become,

and more, a tiny blue
crown for nothing's
feckless king,
the drunken soul
through alcohol
lit up posthumously
like a word.

And finally, he wants
no more than in a moment
to forever stall
and mix these contents,
and to drink the wet gold
and violet pulp.

"ON LANGUAGE" ATTEMPTS TO DESCRIBE THE INABILITY OF LANGUAGE TO SEPARATE ITSELF FROM emotion, especially during the exasperating political and social arena of Bucharest in 1981.

After realizing that my apartment had been searched, and that I was receiving impersonating phone calls (a way of monitoring the Romanian poets I was translating), I left my residence (on Boulevard Pionilior) in disgust, only to realize that I was being followed by two rather shabby secret service police. I had left my apartment with the particular desire to write.

Later, after having lost my "two secret literary enthusiasts," I attempted, out of frustration, to write something. It was evening, I was sitting by a pond, and a full moon, breaking through the clouds, had risen over a large billboard which read in the distance: "Long Live the Communist Party."

An intermittent rain began to fall, and after writing for an hour I destroyed the beginnings of the poem that I would write again, two years later. At that particular moment the only language "not ineffable" seemed to be fire, water, and to a lesser, or greater extent, the Stolichnaya vodka, its brief, faltering monument—"a tiny blue/crown for nothing's/feckless king."

For a Long Time I Have Wanted to Write a Happy Poem

> *Between two worlds life hovers like a star.*
> — Byron

It is not so easy to live on the earth
as an angel, to imitate the insects that dance
around the moon, to return what air we borrow
every few seconds. I am going to enter
the hour when wind dreamt of a light dress
to stroke, when water dreamt of the lips it would meet.
The famous Pascalian worm will just have to find
another heart to eat.
I will reveal the actual reason birds fly off
so suddenly from telephone wires.
The road will ask my foot for help.
The lightening will forget its thunder.
I will discover the hidden planet
to account for Pluto's eccentric orbit.
Pluto, of course, is ready to leave the alliance.
No longer will I have to lament
the death of Mary, the circus elephant,
hung with chains from a derrick on Sept. 16, 1916,
in Erwin, Tennessee, to punish her immortal soul
for brushing her keeper to death.
She looks out from her daguerreotype
as if she knows one day we too will hear
the stars gnaw away at our darkness.
It is not so easy.
One day I will free the clouds frozen in ponds.
No longer will the wind lose its way.
I will start hearing important voices like a real saint.
The Emir of Kuwait will answer my call.
If I am not careful I will loosen

the noose of history from around my own neck.
Just to keep sane I will have to include my weight
which is the only thing that keeps me from being a bird.
Walking on air will no longer be a problem.
Meanwhile, the Hubble telescope is still wobbling
its pictures from outer space so we will
have to rely on imagination a little longer to see clearly.
Why don't windows tell us everything they see?
Here come the characters of my sad poems.
They have been standing in line to get in
like fans at a rock concert.
They are gathering around Beatrix Potter who spent 30 years
locked in her room. The maid brings up her supper.
She sneaks out into the garden to capture
small animals to draw or reinvent before they die.
Beatrix, I say, we no longer have to kill what we see.
I know this in my heart, in my wolf, in my owl.
In the Siena of my palms. The Bergamo of my head.
In the garlic of my fingers. My friends say
I use too much. There are never enough
streets crossing the one we are stuck on.
No one wants to be a cloud anymore.
Who still believes in the transmigration of souls?
If you believe Bell's theorem, then the fact is
that the squirrel falling out of my tree this morning
makes minute sub-atomic changes from here to Australia.
Will I have to put on my pants differently now?
Just when we start to believe in moonlight
we notice how many stars it erases. It is not easy.
I am going to come back
as the birthmark on the inside of your thigh,
between your dreams of angels and solar dust,
between your drunken skirt and the one that laughs.
I am going to learn what the butterfly knows
about disguise, what so astonishes the hills.
All this is going to take constant vigilance.
In *The Last Chance Saloon*, Tombstone, Arizona,
I saw the lizard creature with its glued head,
almost human, tilted up from under the glass,
as if it didn't know which world to claim.
Apparently it fooled a lot of people in 1872.
I kept thinking if only Ovid had seen this creature
he would have known his nymphs

could never escape just by turning into trees.
In Dora Noar, Afghanistan, the young soldier,
Mohammad Anwar, age 13, believes he will turn
into a desert flower when he dies in the vihad.
The barrel of his AK-47 is sawed down
because he is small as the four prisoners
he has returned with. They understand
that all we know of the sky we learn by listening to roots.
I was happy, he says after shooting them
against a wall, over and over again, *I was happy*.
Happy. Now maybe the earth will want to change its name.
It won't want to be the earth anymore.
Shadows will be abandoned by their objects.
The light will squander itself on the flowers
because they do not even want to be flowers anymore.
It is not easy to live on this earth.
We don't understand that the universe is
blowing away from us like litter,
but at an incredible speed.
There is a new theory that the universe is left-handed.
It has to do with the spin of quarks.
Someone else says it's in the form of a horseshoe.
The rest of the animal is metamorphosed into a black hole.
I happen to side with the fanatics who believe
it is following the call of a mythic bird too distant to see,
but this is only poetry, like the old papers
the homeless use to stuff their clothes on cold nights,
the kind of poetry that says, flowers, be happy,
trees, raise your drooping eyebrows,
sky, don't turn your back on us again,
my love, how wonderful to have lived while you lived,
which is not the sort of poetry you read anyplace anymore.

The Poet as Happy Fatalist

WHEN I WAS YOUNGER I READ MORE FICTION THAN POETRY. DIEDEROT'S *JACQUES THE FATALIST* with its several narrators, its diversions, interruptions, false starts, its purposely inadequate conclusions, its poetics of not taking the world seriously, could have been a model, a very serious model. So I think of the poem as a dance of Stevens' Macabre Mice. A masked ball where the costumes are all switched around. Which leads to one line calling another which pretends, for a while, not to hear. Or hears the wrong thing. Remember those carnival grab bags where for a nickel you might get something worthless and frivolous or something of great value? You have to love them both. It's not what you get, it's being able to pick.

Jean Janzen

Potato Planting

All you need is one good eye,
he said in the still chilly spring,
his spade making soft, black holes.

The cut pieces soon stir
with that nourishing fire
like those losses we think

we bury for good, that begin
to smolder in their dark sleep
and extend their thin, white roots.

What is visible flourishes.
Under the glare of the sun
potato plants push out

their rough tongues and make
their easy promises. Not until
the fall digging do we see them,

whole families of pale,
forgotten children coming home
at dusk, blackened

by the coal mines, waiting
to be washed and held,
begging for their stories to be told.

WE WORK IN THE DARK. THE WRITING IS A DIG. NOTHING NEW, REALLY, EXCEPT SOMETIMES the smell of earth as discoveries are made. This poem feels true to my writing experience. The common metaphors for poets in the common act give me a sense of connectedness that enriches me. My writing has moved me to the stories of my ancestors and of others, creating a wider, more fertile field. I plant them for continuity and nurture, and out of an internal necessity. The vision is partial, even as I long for the elemental, a singularity of sight that multiplies.

What Only Poetry Can Do

What is it only poetry can do?
This: I am nine years old. My father lowers
Me down into the dungeon of a castle
In Fife, and follows after. On the walls
Are grooves licked by the tongues of prisoners.
A broken wall reveals the Firth of Forth,
Blue under open sky, and our way out.
This was the castle of Macduff. At nine,
I knew he had beheaded King Macbeth
In Shakespeare's play, a play of blood and ghosts.

At thirty-seven, driving west in Fife,
Along the Firth of Forth, I found the place
Again, exactly where it stood before,
But blocked now by a modern cemetery.
On the ruined keep—a splash of vandalism.
When I walked out past the graves, along a cliff
Falling away like rotten scaffolding,
On an upper level, clinging to a fence,
A man called, "Hoy!" to stop me. And I stopped.

THE FIRST LINE OF "WHAT ONLY POETRY CAN DO" CAME TO ME AFTER I HAD FINISHED WRITing a book-length narrative poem that had taken three years to complete. It was 1990 and I had spent the past decade trying to write poems that told stories. I believed that poetry could perform this ancient art, one of its original functions, as well as prose fiction. The pursuit had finally exhausted me and I began asking myself the question, "What is it only poetry can do?"

I had been living in England for the past year and had been able to return to that part of Scotland where I had lived as a child. I subjected my patient family to a number of returns to childhood landmarks, including Macduff Castle on the road between East and West Wymess in Fife. In order to answer my question, I tried writing about that visit and one I had made to the castle with my father almost thirty years before.

I think there are times when the events in our lives have the sort of symmetry we try to create in a poem. It is easier to see their shape when looking back, of course, and the passage of time is also more conducive to making fiction, if that is necessary. Still, as I recalled exploring the ruins of Macduff Castle with my father and the way I had been unable to enter them again as an adult, I thought if I could render both events clearly and set them side by side, I would have a poem.

But is the question, "What is it only poetry can do?", answered by the two stanzas I finally wrote? Each stanza is a narrative, after all. In sequence they offer a simple chronology, albeit with a lengthy hiatus suggested by the band of white space that separates them. If I wanted to show there was something poetry could do that prose could not, it was certainly not going to be by telling stories again.

I wanted to return to the compression of the lyric, but I had to do it wearing my narrative gear. I wanted to return to that small space, like the dungeon of Macduff Castle, that could open, as its broken wall did, into larger possibilities. I wanted to show that the beauty of the lyric, or just the short poem, was in knowing when to stop. I wanted to rediscover that sense of tact. Compression, brevity, and tact were, I believed, three things that only a poem could achieve.

Later, I learned there was another way to read the poem and another answer to my question. The poet Christopher Buckley told me he understood exactly what I meant. "What only poetry can do," he said, "is go back." In this particular case, poetry allowed me not only to venture into the past but to bring it back to the present. Poetry could represent both what I could not physically do, which was return to being nine years old, and what I physically encountered when I tried to revisit a place that change had made inaccessible. Poetry crossed boundaries of time and space that I could not cross any other way. It did what only poetry can do.

⸓⸎

Judy Jensen

Faith

Look at her. It's not even six and she's already struggling
up the hill near my house. Her face is blacker than the cold
morning air clamped around her as she heaves her weight
forward to her job as cleaning lady or laundress or cook.
It doesn't matter what she does. She's got what she's got
and that's more than some. Still, I want to tell her
what I know. In Ahmadi, the oil fields still burn.
The Emir's royal garden is silent under a coat
of heavy slime that mutes the signed language of the leaves.
The Iraqis ate the antelope and deer that roamed
within the walls. Rotting carcasses and bones lay in piles
like torn knapsacks and discarded weapons beside the stable.
But where are the horses, she might ask. Or she might not.
She's got what she's got and she might not be interested
in anything other than what it takes to keep it. But some mornings,
it can be hard to rise from the bed knowing that each new day will play
out like the last. One more layer of dust, one more crisp shirt
swinging in white surrender, the usual for the suit sitting
at the counter with his Wall Street Journal. Money evaporates
faster than a downpour in a desert. And so I want to tell her
about my friend Max, how he left home for the first time.
How he drove from Philly to Tucson and had forgotten
the envelope of money his dad gave him at Bookbinders.
How sixteen hours later, in Tucumcari, hungry and tired,
he stopped at a quick mart for a soda and a hot dog he bought
with loose change he scraped from the floor of his car.

73

How he walked out into a light wind, a rustling breeze that sent
a twenty dollar bill spiraling past his nose, one after another
after another. Max plucked them out of the gasoline-scented air,
raked them up like leaves off the asphalt. Where did
the money come from, she might ask. Or she might not.
She may not have time for such foolishness. When workday's
over, but there's still the kids' homework and dinner
to get through and her man doesn't have any clean
shirts for tomorrow. Or there is no man, no family.
Just her job, its boredom cutting into her like a saddle.
So who cares where the money came from? Max didn't.
He probably wouldn't care about the horses in Kuwait
or the violets in my yard either. Early October. I was walking
back to my spent vegetable bed to clear out dry tomato stalks,
to cut back the peppermint and thyme when I spotted
violets blooming beneath the heart-shaped shields of leaves.
Shy drops of amethyst against brown velvet. I remember it
as clearly as the photos and film footage of the oil wells torched
by the soldiers as they fled, an inferno of howling red haze
and stinging black defeat. In the Emir's aviary, all that's left
of the peacocks are the clumps of feathers on the ground.
There were thirty-two Arabians in the Emir's stable.
Some were taken to Baghdad, others starved, some found
in the desert with their throats slit. But two months later,
four of the horses were found alive, wandering in the heart
of the burning fields, oil soaked and wary behind eyes
rimmed with black soot. This is what I want to tell
the woman as she struggles up the hill. They are only
stories. And little ones at that. But what more
do we have to wrap around ourselves in the cold?

I HAD THE CLIPPING IN MY KITCHEN FOR ALMOST TWO YEARS: "DEFYING ODDS, FOUR
HORSES SURVIVE INFERNO IN KUWAIT." I knew it was a trigger for something, but two years
passed and I still had not gotten past a few false starts. I laid it aside but never forgot about
it. Finally, some incidents occurred within a couple of weeks and set the poem in motion.
     During an unusually bitter cold spell, I kept passing the same woman on the road on
my way into work and a friend told me about leaving home for the first time, a story that
he swore he had told me years ago. I felt like I'd been handed the poem on a platter. It
practically wrote itself. This poem pleases me for the firsts it represents. It's the first time
I've moved beyond the simple lyrical poem to weave seemingly disparate elements into
one whole. It's also the first time I've looked beyond my own personal experiences to find
subject matter. The burning oil fields could have been approached politically or environ-
mentally but the horses gave me the opportunity to approach this unnatural disaster from
a uniquely humane perspective and to see the natural disaster of a life lived unrealized.

The Bridge

These fulsome sounds, these abbreviations of the air,
Are not real, but two of them may get a small man
I knew in high school, who, seeing an accident,
Stopped one day, leapt over a mangled guard rail,
Took a mother and two children from a flooded creek,
And lifted them back to the world. In the dark,
I do not know, there is no saying, but he pulled
Them each up a tree, which was not the tree of life,
But a stooped Alabama willow, flew three times
From the edge of that narrow bridge as though
From the selfless shore of a miracle and came back
To the false name of a real man, Arthur Peavahouse.
He could sink a set shot from thirty feet. One night
I watched him field a punt and a scat behind a wall
Of blockers like a butterfly hovering an outhouse.
He did not love the crashing of bodies. He
Did not know that mother and her three children,
But went down one breath to their darkness.
There is no name for that place, you cannot
Find them following a white chain of bubbles
Down the muddy water of these words. But I saw
Where the rail sheared from the bridge—which is
Not real since it was replaced by a wider bridge.
Arthur Peavahouse weighed a hundred and twenty pounds.
Because he ran well in the broken field, men
Said he was afraid. I remember him best
At a laboratory table, holding a test tube
Up to the light, arranging equations like facts,
But the school is air over a parking lot. You
Are too far from that valley for it to come
All the way true, although it is not real.
Not two miles from that bridge, one afternoon
In March, in 1967, one of my great uncles,
Clyde Maples, a farmer and a Commissioner of Roads,
And his neighbor, whose name I have forgotten,
Pulled more than a hundred crappie off three
Stickups in that creek—though the creek is not
Real and the valley a valley of words. You
Would need Clyde Maples to find Arthur Peavahouse,
And you would need Clyde Maples' side yard
Of roadgraders and bulldozers to get even part
Of Clyde Maples, need him like the crappies
Needed those stickups in the creek to tell them
Where they were. Every spring that creek
Darkens with the run-off of hog-lots and barns,
Spreading sloughs, obscuring sorghum and corn.
On blind backwater full schoolbuses roll

Down buried roads. Arthur Peavahouse was smart
To run from the huge tackles and unthinking
To throw himself into that roiling water
And test the reality of his arms and his lungs.
Many times I have thought everything I have said
Or thought was a lie, moving some blame or credit
By changing a name, even the color of a lip or bush,
But whenever I think of the lie that stands for truth,
I think of Arthur Peavahouse, and not his good name,
But him deciding, as that car settled to the bottom,
To break free and live for at least one more moment
Upward toward light and the country of words
While the other child, the one he could not save,
Shrugged behind him in the unbreakable harness.

Some Ramblings on "The Bridge"

IN ALL MY WORK WITH LANGUAGE, I HAVE BEEN OBSESSED BY CONTRADICTION, BELIEVING ON
the one hand, that language has a duty to authenticate experience, and, on the other hand,
that language is, first and foremost, an intimation of character. I am trapped, bound, and
determined to honor and transcend this situation. In doing this, I try to recognize the pol-
itics of language, that every word that engages me bears the tracks of its previous users,
and is both an exhibition of loyalty and a battle-cry that alerts others to inexplicable enmi-
ty. Nevertheless, I would be drawn into a deeper encounter, to that place where the direc-
tion of the poem is less determined by logical preconceptions than by the possibilities
inherent in the rhythmical and melodic flow of the language, for I believe that the art may
have beauty insofar as its practitioners allow that the sound of a word may nourish the cry
or song of a creature whose most essential nature is incapable of linguistic expression.

I would rather just accept this duality of language, but, in our time, it seems to me
that not just the natural world but an aesthetics of language has been bruised somewhat
by its continual subjugation to utility. It is not just the periodic calls to minimalism or the
remonstrations of this or that critic to abandon the clutter of personal experience in favor
of some more orderly commitment to the spirit of community. There is the need to tear
every poem apart, not to see how its artistry was affected, but to reveal the hubris of its
maker, and thus, to render it, not in terms of artistry, but in terms of the central mean-
inglessness of an ego that seeks to impose on the reader an act of power. To look at a poem
in the same way that one looks at an advertisement for Cap'n Crunch or a political speech
is tantamount to looking at a living animal in the same way that one looks at a video
recording machine.

It embarrasses me to admit that my writing of "The Bridge" was fueled by my anger
at those readers who seek to reduce the art to the strutting of ego, but that was, in fact, the
case. My intuition in "The Bridge" was simple: to tear down the poem as I constructed it,
to reveal the shabbiness of its materials, and, hopefully, by doing that, to emphasize an act
that had little to do with language but with the heroism of an actual man, Arthur
Peavahouse. And now that it is done, I might wish that I were a different poet, more pure-
ly consumed by the task of working a kind of music into speech that is at once believable
and remarkable, and less concerned with the immediate environment of poetry, but it
seems to me that, in the direct encounter, I had no choice. Neither, I believe, did the other
poets in this anthology. It is popular to speak of poetry in the abstract, and often students
have asked me what I think poetry will be like twenty years from now, but I would prefer
to think that any answer I might give would prove inadequate, for I am sure that such an
art as poetry will always depend on the issue of one ungovernable heart.

Ars Poetica

I will go home
when my mother dies,
finger her jewelry, drape
her many scarves 'round
and 'round my head,
pack the last
of her smell into boxes.
Her cupid lamps
I will sell, her paintings
burn. I will not find any letters.

The glass animals
gazing serenely from my kitchen sill
shatter one by one.
Upon waking,
the sun grazes
my face.
The dust in the air
blazes into sight.
I raise her lips to my cup.
I ask the day to keep me.

"Ars Poetica" was written at a time when I was grappling with my lifetime love for the literature of exile. I'd been reading James Joyce and Milan Kundera and was increasingly uneasy in my reading. In the deeply sexual beauty of their sentences, I read an ultimately unfaithful negotiation with the temporal world. Stephen Daedalus' decision—which Joyce used again and again in various guises as *the* 20th century notion of freedom—not to return to Ireland when his mother died remained merely an aesthetic choice, one alive only in the writing, one removed from the life lived, and thus, for me, a false, or rather, a non-choice. And Kundera's notion of "lightness" in *The Unbearable Lightness of Being*—really, I asked the pages, is that really it? The urgencies of these men, removed as they were from the very literal body of their countries, remained adolescent, rooted in a narcissistic recognition of self. Give me the terseness of Miroslav Holub, that eye to the microscope; give me the attack of a writer like Vaclav Havel. Let me find the courage to write the decaying body of my country *in* my country, which for the poet is the word, the true word.

"Ars Poetica" wishes to negate the refuge of form.

Yusef Komunyakaa

Safe Subjects

How can love heal
the mouth shut this way?
Say something worth breath.
Let it surface, recapitulate
how fat leeches press down
gently on a sex goddess's eyelids.
Let truth have its way with us
like a fishhook holds
to life, holds dearly to nothing
worth saying—pull it out,
bringing with it hard facts,
knowledge that the fine underbone
of hope is also attached
to inner self, underneath it all.
Undress. No, don't be afraid
even to get Satan mixed up in this
acknowledgement of thorns:
meaning there's madness
in the sperm, in the egg,
fear breathing in its blood sac,
true accounts not so easily
written off the sad book.

Say something about pomegranates.
Say something about real love.
Yes, true love—more than
parted lips, than parted legs
in sorrow's darkroom of potash
& blues. Let the brain stumble
from its hidingplace, from its cell block,
to the edge of oblivion
to come to itself, sharp-tongued
as a boar's grin in summer moss
where a vision rides the back
of God, at this masquerade.
Redemptive as a straight razor
against a jugular vein—
unacknowledged & unforgiven.
It's truth we're after here,
hurting for, out in the streets
where my brothers kill each other,
each other's daughters & guardian angels
in the opera of dead on arrival.

Say something that resuscitates
us, behind the masks,
as we stumble off into neon nights
to loveless beds & a second skin
of loneliness. Something political as dust
& earthworms at work in the temple
of greed & mildew, where bowed lamps
cast down shadows like blueprints of graves.
Say something for us who can't believe
in the creed of nightshade.
Yes, say something to us dreamers
who decode the message of dirt
between ancient floorboards
as black widow spiders
lay translucent eggs
in the skull of a dead mole
under a dogwood in full bloom.

Forces that Move the Spirit: Duende and Blues

WHEN FEDERICO GARCIA LORCA TALKS ABOUT DUENDE, THE INFLUENCE OF ANDALUSIAN Gypsies on his poetry, how they shaped the concept of *cante jondo*, I feel that he's talking about a similar, if not the same, emotional soil from which has sprung the blues. I think of Son House, Leadbelly, Charley Patton, Ma Rainey, Blind Lemon Jefferson, etc., with the Mississippi as a slow-motion backdrop. I think of the delta's rich bottomland, the sweat and blood that have gone into endless rituals of survival, the brute force and almost obscene beauty of its peasantry, and how the music and songs are closer to prayers than anything else—an earthy atticism. If one can squeeze love out of these songs, he can taste distilled mercy. Or terror. Here's a class of people refusing to lie down and be counted as victims.

Willie Dixon says that "The whole of life itself expresses the blues. That's why I always say the blues are the true facts of life expressed in words and song, inspiration, feeling and understanding." Indeed, the blues are existential. They are also black and basic. And it is this down-to-earthness that I hope informs the main tenor of my poetry—a language that deals with the atrabilious nature of our existence, as well as the emotional weight of its beauty. This is what Lorca saw in the *cante jondo*. Apparently, the Gypsy singer Manuel Torre said in 1922, as Manuel de Falla played *Nights in the Gardens of Spain*, that "Whatever has black sounds has *duende*." The sounds of the soil, of the earth turning around in its monumental mystery—conception and birth sounds that stumble out of the night, the violent serenity that Jean Toomer attempted to capture in *Cane*, and the fact that for one to embrace such moments is antithetical to the European psyche and its classic fear of the unknown.

I love the raw lyricism of the blues. Its mystery and conciseness. I admire and cherish how the blues singer attempts to avoid abstraction; he makes me remember that balance and rhythm keep our lives almost whole. The essence of mood is also important here. Mood becomes a directive; it becomes the bridge that connects us to who we are philosophically and poetically. Emotional texture is drawn from the aesthetics of insinuation and nuance. But to do this well the poet has to have a sense of history. Of course this often means that one has to reeducate oneself. James Baldwin talks about having taken recordings of Bessie Smith to Sweden to begin to recreate where he came from before he could write *Another Country*—the natural tongue of his beginnings. Perhaps he desired only a certain mood. I agree with this analysis of Janheinz Jahn's: "The blues do not arise from a mood, but produce one. Like every art form in African culture, song too is an attitude which affects something. The spiritual produces God, the secularized blues produce a mood."

The mood I desire in my poetry is one in which the truth can survive. I love satire. How the Fool operates in *King Lear* is brilliant: He is the wise man in the midst of a cultivated system of evasions and self-deception. Likewise, often the blues singer can get us closer to truth than the philosopher. This is the function of my poetry.

⌒❀❀❀⌒

Maxine Kumin

Ars Poetica: A Found Poem

Whenever I caught him down in the stall, I'd approach.
At first he jumped up the instant he heard me slide
the bolt. Then I could get the door open while
he stayed lying down, and I'd go in on my hands
and knees and crawl over to him so that
I wouldn't appear so threatening. It took
six or eight months before I could simply walk in
and sit with him, but I needed that kind of trust.

I kept him on a long rein to encourage him
to stretch out his neck and back. I danced with him
over ten or fifteen acres of fields with a lot
of flowing from one transition to another.
What I've learned is how to take the indirect route.
That final day I felt I could have cut
the bridle off, he went so well on his own.

THE CREDIT FOR THIS POEM RESTS WITH DAVID O'CONNOR OF UPPERVILLE, VIRGINIA, A world-class equestrian; the poem is based on his own account of working with a very talented but troubled horse. It struck me that we do much the same sort of work with poems in process. That is to say, we struggle to establish some sort of rapport with the subject, we dance with it, flowing from one transition to another, and if we are ultimately very lucky, the poem comes into its own. It helps, of course, to know horses and it especially helps to have experienced that moment of exquisite balance detailed in the last two lines of the poem, but I hope that even without special equestrian skills a reader can make the identification.

⌒❀❀❀⌒

Ann Lauterbach

Poem

If only it were a matter of wet strawberries
among wet lettuces, or the mauve gray haze
on the road north. The decors
rush in and we are sated by looking
but there are other colorations, other codes.
There were frogs all over the airport.
There was nothing around but France.
And there are the nights when a long caress
breaks through the film of sleep
yielding something unspeakably true.

I wanted to say, "All I want inside is you."
I did not, because you are not
all that I want. If I insist, and I do,
on always including you, it is because
I foresee no other anchor when things are
so windy and culpable. We must return to the day
we were shattered into care, even
with the severe things going on in front of us.

EACH POEM WE WRITE MANIFESTS ITS OWN RECIPE, OR INTENT; IT REVEALS, WE HOPE, ITS process which in turn is included in the next poem. In time, a sense of weaving occurs; we recognize what we do. This poem, the first in my first collection, *Many Times, But Then* (University of Texas Press 1979), now tells me of certain traits or ingredients or structures that are indicative of how I think about writing.

The trope of the visual, external world, the world as depiction, is placed in relation to the world as sound, as inscription. Naming the world through the eye is, I am beginning to think, tied to the idea of consumption: when we name what we see we take possession of it. I am beginning to think of it as a "masculine" way of entering discourse. The world construed through the ear is the world received and recessed; it is the place of listening; I am beginning to think this is a "feminine" way of knowing. The poem is constructed through both agencies, not in opposition, but in tandem.

The coherence of the poem is built from a series of fragments; but the fragment is, in itself, a whole thing, not a piece of a prior whole. The idea of the fragment as a complete gesture in itself (as motif), came, I think, from noticing how important the stroke of a brush is in painting, particularly in abstract painting—think of Agnes Martin, or David Reed; think, obviously, of Jackson Pollock. Each stroke constitutes a moment of making, and is complete in or to itself. The poem builds a narrative from these discrete gestures which, in turn, arise from disparate sources. (In urban life, we are constantly made aware of how narratives are artificial, imposed on the world through the myriad actions of the world.)

To survive we must construe meaning; we are dependent, we are attached. The poem declares the importance of attachment—to each other, to language as world. We are "shattered into care" and each shard conditions our grasp of particulars, or need for inclusion, and the erotics of desire that propel us to go on saying what we know in order to find out what we do not yet know. The poem unfurls this dialogue with the unknown, placing new narrative fields on the haphazard, the unexpected, the "windy and culpable." We are accountable to its song.

Accident

Never to remember
New York City
Mingus's splendid tirades
Chico   Max
The MJQ   or early Gerry
He rides
His bike shooting out of woods like a switchblade
Onto the lane
In our meadow where night air
Leaves a slick on the gravel. This dawn
Has no steam breathing through pavement cobbles
But a purple moth struggles
With the wet burden like Elvin
Jones in a gin-soaked club
And with his half-shucked shell
Into such brief improvisation
Of beauty that if the boy were nearer
Or it were an hour later
(Daytime frogs on the beat
Like morning cops—Ninth at Broadway, dawn,
Twenty years gone—
Or my daughter doing her scat
Voices drowning
The riff of wings like tiny high-hat cymbals)
I would never have noticed

The muted sun like Miles cut through
The mistflumes' chorus
On the river where mayflies
Lose their shifting hold on pebbles
At the bottom and make their way up
And trout at their stations hover like trebles
In the haysweet hills
The I I think I am
Beats against the snare of the past
And sleep and dream
Hard case
My son repeats
The terrible solo again
And again in his seventh summer
That decrescendo
Dreaming his bike a flyer
Set for the moon like Diz
Last night my baby daughter
Poked a thumb at the ofay moon
And sang, "I want it." She thinks

It's Big Rock Candy. Meatfat and drink
Clash in my sour intestines
Like Monk's odd clusters at the old Half Note
The moth flies up
And clings in splendor to a screen

Hanging in country air
There's a boy's high wail
As his fender shivers like a tambourine

I'M COMPELLED BY FROST'S NOTION OF THE POEM AS A STAY AGAINST CONFUSION, SINCE I
believe my existence would be a jumble without recourse to writing verse. For whatever
its quality, my poetry is a means to discover connections among my heart's responses.
Things, ideas, emotions: these arrive to me as to anyone in no order nor integrity; if
they're to have any shapeliness at all, it will be "poetical." My ars poetica must be my ars
vita and vice-versa. To adore my wife and children is to imagine my life with them as an
ongoing poem, this being my aptest metaphor for every worthwhile thing I do.

I've never set out to make a poem about poetry. In truth, despite the glorious exam-
ples of a Stevens or a Williams, such efforts often bore me. Yet each of my poems is
inevitably about *being* a poet, that self-definition charging all my earthly relations and—
since I call myself Christian—my super-earthly.

The first thing I want to say about "Accident," no matter its palpable melancholy, is
that the poem's not gloomy. I impute to it rather the spirit of a Wordsworth passage
(even if it contradicts Frost's formula): "I could wish my days to be/ Bound each to each
by natural piety." My "nature" poems aim especially to find such continuity; but this one
finds it too, at least partly.

And accidentally: one August dawn in 1979, I walked outdoors, passing first through
my woodshed, from which a moth, numb with unseasonable cold, struggled to fly. The
night before, I'd heard a radio feature on Charles Mingus, and my head was full of his
music. I couldn't think of Mingus without recalling his public chastisement of my
untimely applause—as he considered it—at a 1961 performance in the East Village. All
these years later, my first son was just learning to ride a bike, and as I looked out on the
meadow where he practiced, it occurred to me that—reared in the boondocks—he'd
never have so specifically urban a memory as that one of mine. But I forgot all this, of
course, when he took his nasty spill.

I did not, however, forget it long. When I went to my desk, the '60's New York jazz
scene, the moth, and the accident all crowded my mind, emotional stuff in each. I decid-
ed—as my ars poetica requires—to dig for their commonalty.

The very word "accident" quickly proved helpful. Given its Latin root (*accidens*), I
surmised that while listening to Mingus I'd experienced beauties "falling toward" me. I
knew also that "accidentals" were notes outside the key signature of a given composition,
of which notes there were plenty in Mingus-era jazz. It struck me that on this later morn-
ing other beauties had likewise fallen, that they were forcing my soul out of *its* quotidi-
an key (plain C), and even its tempo (a staltwart 4/4).

Yes, I felt sadness for the moth, like us all so ephemeral; and for Mingus, silenced by
the sclerosis that would soon kill him; and of course for my mildly wounded son. Yet as
I wrote the world seemed suddenly tuneful and I blessed—blessed above all to have a
poet's life. If like anyone I'd often witnessed "brief improvisation[s] of beauty," I'd also
been able to protract their span. On the page. And this morning there was, as always,
other luck too: I could have come out through the kitchen and not the woodshed; my boy
could have been shooting baskets and not riding a bike; had I listened to a Red Sox game
rather than a jazz program, box scores and not music might have been on my mind.

As every parent will understand, it was above all the bicycle mishap—dramatizing my child's plain, human vulnerability—that brought thoughts of the passage of time, the certainty of mortality, the very improvisatory quality of our lives, all of which might have spun my brain. Yet I had at least the momentary means to stay such confusion.

In "Accident," "The I I think I am/ beats against the snare of the past"; that self fears discontinuity between now and then, not to mention between a father's experience and the experience of his flesh and blood, seeming so recklessly downhill on wobbly wheels. But the poem at last seems able to impose an integrity on pain, loss, joy, and beauty, to bind them each to each. If the world fast-forwards from past to present, and is rife with other disparities as well, there are moments when it proceeds somehow to harmony, when even falling may seem an ascent. To record these instants—I close with another Frostian echo—is at least temporarily to "be whole again beyond confusion."

<hr />

Carol Lem

Ars Poetica

Who is it that sits beside me,
who talks to me in shadows,
who wakes to this page
scratching in silence?

At night she opens a familiar book,
inhaling the dark crisp leaves.
She hears the first rain of fall,
as the sky breaks like a thousand veins
and no one here to comfort
the small hurts bleeding on the page.

The house shakes
with the rumble of trains.
She thinks what if
it is the earth or the next war,
bodies float to shore anyway.
Somehow, they fill the bag
she drags from line to line.
At the desk she searches for survivors,
gives them a name, a place
I can find them.

The trees are bare now
and spring seems so far away.
Don't worry, they'll return
without you, she says,
you have only this now, then
gives me a word.

Poem as Meditation

WHEN PEOPLE ASK WHERE DO YOUR POEMS COME FROM?, I USUALLY TELL A STORY THAT GOES something like this: I grew up in a house where no one *talked* to each other. I spent a lot of time in my room, reading into the heart of darkness, following the ends and beginnings of things. I was Prufrock scuttling across the floors of silent seas. Along the path I gathered the usual hurts and losses, no more and I'm sure much less than others I knew whose psyches were being shaped by the Sixties when nothing connected with nothing, or so it seemed. I remember hours in the garage painting images on canvas, until my brother cautioned not to confuse art with protest. One stroke, color balances the other to form a harmonized whole. I understood, but too much was happening. The anti-war movement brought the poets out. Even the peace candidate Eugene McCarthy, a poet, was reading at rallies. I began writing poems as a way of expressing my disharmony. Unity of being would come later.

With the passing years, I eventually realized what my brother meant as the poem, the shards of living, and solitude forced me into the rooms of my own making where I could explore this "I" my mother named Carol because she loved Christmas carols and my father Mei Ling to please his father. To this day, I identify with small rooms, garages, the solitary places, remembering things past, ordering the sights, sounds, the smells within—the backyard plum tree, my father's abacus, Sunday's pot pork, my mother calling me in to eat, the fragments of conversation that merge with the years as past becomes present, and the future a riddle of images yet to be.

The poems come out of this need to connect with the *other* if only for a half hour in the morning. Making a poem is meditation, like playing the shakuhachi or doing zazen. The process tames the monkey mind, so I can hear what my secret sharer is thinking, feeling. It is a way of staying in touch with her fears, griefs, desires. The demands of everyday life seem, at times, to conspire against these moments together. But the one who sits beside me keeps calling me in, if only to be here in readiness, receptivity to what she had to give me.

There are many you's in my poems because of this need to *talk* when I can't in the conventional way. Death or the daily masks prevent *meeting*. William Carlos Williams says it best, "Be patient that I address you in a poem,/there is no other/ fit medium." And Emily Dickinson whose poems are letters to the world.

A morning's meditation may not yield many lines, but I am here, and always something is given, even it it's silence, to this traveler who asks is there anybody here and finds herself a host of phantom listeners. Midway through my journey it is enough to come, enough to keep my word.

Philip Levine

The Simple Truth

I bought a dollar and a half's worth of small red potatoes,
took them home, boiled them in their jackets
and ate them for dinner with a little butter and salt.
Then I walked through the dried fields
on the edge of town. In middle June the light
hung on in the dark furrows at my feet,
and in the mountain oaks overhead the birds
were gathering for the night, the jays and mockers
squawking back and forth, the finches still darting
into the dusty light. The woman who sold me
the potatoes was from Poland; she was someone
out of my childhood in a pink spangled sweater and sunglasses
praising the perfection of all her fruits and vegetables
at the road-side stand and urging me to taste
even the pale, raw sweet corn trucked all the way,
she swore, from New Jersey. "Eat, eat," she said,
"Even if you don't I'll say you did."
                                        Some things
you know all your life. They are so simple and true
they must be said without elegance, meter and rhyme,
they must be laid on the table beside the salt shaker,
the glass of water, the absence of light gathering
in the shadows of picture frames, they must be
naked and alone, they must stand for themselves.
My friend Henri and I arrived at this together in 1965
before I went away, before he began to kill himself,
and the two of us to betray our love. Can you taste
what I'm saying? It is onions or potatoes, a pinch
of simple salt, the wealth of melting butter, it is obvious,
it stays there for the rest of your life, unspoken,
made of that dirt we call earth, the metal we call salt,
in a form we have no words for, and you live on it.

DID RAY ROBINSON HAVE A VISION OF WHY BOXING MATTERED AND A NOTION OF HOW IT
should be practiced? I would doubt it, although after a time I'm sure he knew from expe-
rience it required the best his mind and body could give, and I'm sure he worked very
hard so they could give their best. The night he took the middleweight title from Jake
LaMotta he must have known that all his work and his talent had come together at the
perfect moment, and he was the greatest fighter in the world: he knew all there was about
his art, and he acted on that knowledge. Such is the nature of genius. In another key,
Dickinson often must have felt a similar command of her faculties, and Stevens as well.
I live in a different world, perhaps the same world grass lives in, and at certain times I
grow and green without the least notion of why one day is different from another.
Afterwards I'm amazed at what I've done and feel victorious without having defeated
anything or anyone. The next morning I'm in the dark working without the least confi-
dence I know anything useful or final about the making of poems.

The Poem You Asked For

My poem would eat nothing.
I tried giving it water
but it said no,

worrying me.
Day after day,
I held it up to the light,

turning it over,
but it only pressed its lips
more tightly together.

It grew sullen, like a toad
through with being teased.
I offered it all my money,

my clothes, my car with a full tank.
But the poem stared at the floor.
Finally I cupped it in

my hands, and carried it gently
out into the soft air, into the
evening traffic, wondering how

to end things between us.
For now it had begun breathing,
putting on more and

more hard rings of flesh.
And the poem demanded the food,
it drank up all the water,

beat me and took my money,
tore the faded clothes
off my back,

said Shit,
and walked slowly away,
slicking its hair down,

Said it was going
over to your place.

I CAN'T THINK OF ANYTHING TO SAY THAT THE POEM, WRITTEN TWENTY-TWO YEARS AGO, hasn't already implied, and, why be redundant?

An ars poetica strikes me as an impossible task just now. I'd rather read Coleridge and the *Biographia Literaria* which is an ars poetica and a work of genius.

I offer the following journal entry: 8/8/92 early a.m. There was this peace I had in working, in writing poems. It made everyone close to me miserable.

Poesia

She props the blue dress shyly over her shoulders,
sheers a pencil line of mascara and smooths blush
over the cheek hot oil scalded to a smeary wax
at four, then high-heels to the dance.
There the girls lull by the band until one
by one the boys pick them.
Aisles and walls empty, a hum of shadows
murmurs by a door, but no one asks her to dance.
No one asks her name.
A few boys, the ones out of school or out of work
look as if . . . but it is always 'as if.'
When she leaves the music stutters to a final note
and lays broken beneath the dancer's feet.
Her best friend Sarah loves her. But even she
reddens to watch the smile that sinks
into a grin, the scar for an eyelash. Finally
she quits going anywhere. When Sarah calls she says
water is boiling, a baby cousin
crying, the TV, important.
But one night, when the house ticks quietly to sleep
and the rooms are a warm darkness, she picks up
the mascara pencil and instead of groceries, writes:
"And her eyes will never know what's equal, one to one."
Then folds towels, lines dishes
and presses clothes for tomorrow.
In bed now, under the reading lamp, she takes the pencil
again, and in one motion, writes:
"The landslide of her face will bury them all in the end."
Then she smiles, the smile seared into a grin;
she blinks the blink sudden as a falling lash,
and knows she will go on, morning will come.

WHEN I THINK OF POETRY, I DON'T THINK OF BORGES' ENDLESS RIVER OR NERUDA'S NIGHT OF infinite substance. I think of a bus driver I once saw pull out a straight razor at two kids harassing him from the presumed safety of their back seats, and before any of those innocent idiots could even beg forgiveness, not to say 'learn a lesson,' he grabbed first one by the hair, phlit . . . phlit, then the other, phlit . . . phlit . . . phlit, and shredded their faces to meat.

At night, sometimes, I think about that bus driver and cringe into my armpits, curl up and thank my lucky milk that he wasn't after me. But he is after me. As is also the woman who must surely be his lover. That vicious wench that smiled across her dashboard after almost deliberately running me over with her car. Even now I hear her tires skewing on the asphalt. Even now I can feel adrenaline scalding through my arteries, and in my mind's eye see her look of sincere malice, her swooning desire to fix my head inside her crotch and squeeze.

A significant part of poetry is for me represented at times by glowering thoughts of hatred, resentment, bitterness and a rapacious desire for revenge. Growing up with a face overly endowed with ugliness, without a voice to whine to weariness my self-pity and feelings of defilement all too commonly felt by poor people of not-the-right-color, I made it my silent task in life and poetry to wreck havoc in some way on those who poisoned my childhood. Oh, weeping tears!

One must remember that to live within and experience poetry in the U.S., especially in the university, is like living in a luxurious suburb, possibly the most penultimate suburb of meaning, where white, European descended poets and their Crayola wannabes can breathe easily and yet at the same time asphyxiate everybody else. They sing with impunity their songs of ourselves while every corpuscle of the world is being burned down to its zinc. I want to say to them, "Get over it!" There's nothing here worth enough to make one degrade oneself by stealing it, or worse, delude oneself into thinking that one will earn it. Refuse the riches, reject the documents.

That is why I am constantly leaving this place of pestilence called "Poetry" in the U.S. and trying to find my way among the insane drivers of the world. I imagine this man, and that woman, possess in abundance what many poets refuse with all their baby-might fists. They are better muses than those rarified hacks we keep digging up to remind ourselves that civilizations may fall, but the very mythologies that brought them down are still okay.

William Matthews

Sad Stories Told in Bars:
The "Reader's Digest" Version

First I was born and it was tough on Mom.
Dad felt left out. There's much I can't recall.
I seethed my way to speech and said a lot
of things: some were deemed cute. I was so small
my likely chance was growth, and so I grew.
Long days in school I filled, like a spring creek,
with boredom. Sex I discovered soon
enough, I now think. Sweet misery!

There's not enough room in a poem so curt
to get me out of adolescence, yet
I'm nearing fifty with a limp, and dread
the way the dead get stacked up like a cord
of wood. Not much of a story, it is?
The life that matters not the one I've led.

Sad Stories and True

HERE ARE THE WORDS TO CAVARADOSSI'S ARIA, "E LUCEVAN LE STELLE" FROM THE THIRD ACT OF Tosca. The translation is William Weaver's.

> and the stars were shining . . .
> and the earth was perfumed,
> the gate of the garden creaked . . .
> and a footstep grazed the sand . . .
> She entered, fragrant,
> she fell into my arms.
> Oh! sweet kisses, oh languid caresses,
> while I impatient
> freed the beautiful form from its veils!
> My dream of love
> vanished forever . . .
> the hour has fled,
> and I die in despair . . .
> and I die in despair!
> And I have never loved life so much . . .
> life so much . . . !

Next, according to the stage directions, Cavaradossi bursts into tears; the aria has reliably had the same effect on me for thirty years.

Cavaradossi believes, and rightly, as it turns out, that he has less than an hour to live, yet it's that hour in the garden he uses the beginnings of his last hour to mourn. "L'ora é fuggita," he sings, but the intensity of that remembered hour brings him both to despair and the most intense love of life he can imagine.

It's possible to be brought to the brink of such intense feeling, I've found, by full rushes of memory, but if I were at the corner of 8th Avenue and 19th Street, let's say, and burst first into the aria and then into tears, I'd clear a rather large space around myself. My fellow New Yorkers would recognize me as a street crazy.

For Cavaradossi it's another matter; people do such things in operas, and besides the poor bastard has but an hour to live. It's the elaboration of the form—signaling a considerable distance from street life—and the lurid melodrama that release the feeling.

Setting the dates and signing the singers for that performance probably took two years. The singers were flown in from an aggregate 20,000 miles. The Tosca sets were fetched from storage, details of lighting and blocking planned, rehearsals worked through. There are some human emotions—central and powerful ones—it's a major project to release.

In "Sad Stories Told in Bars: The 'Reader's Digest' Version," there is, for a fourteen-line poem, considerable work teasing the emotion out. The low-life setting and expectations of self-pity raised by "Sad Stories Told in Bars . . . ," the allusion to the middle-brow Reader's Digest that literary folks love to despise, and the somewhat Mandarin Italian sonnet form all provide, in the tiny way of poems, some distance from the poignancy of the poem's argument, and the tone, veering from falsely jaunty to pluckily morose, suggests the speaker has considerable self-consciousness. But for all that he's in dead earnest.

Maybe that's one of the functions of art, to give us access to emotions so powerful that to consider them all the time would be a mistake: the effort would supplant our routine enjoyment of the world and make Hamlets of us all. But to defer the enjoyment of them—think what pleasure "E lucevan le stelle" can give—until we are, like Cavaradossi, in the literal hour of our death, would be a terrible deprivation.

Colleen J. McElroy

Tapestries

when I was eight I listened to stories of love
and etiquette while my mother's sisters
sat on grandma's horsehair sofa
naked under their starched dresses
words flew from their fingers
in a dance as old as the moon
but I dreamed of other places
of dark bodies bending
to a language too dreamlike
and concise to decode

above them a tapestry desert stretched
into distant corners where I imagined
ancient rituals grotesque and graceful
conjuring up the moon flecked
seasons of the earth
but my mother's sisters wove tales
that collapsed the world
into sarcastic snips of language
their black thighs opened
billows of powdery musk
rising from their legs like dust
from some raw and haunting land

I had a choice
two scenes   their dark secrets
spread for my viewing
the usual desert   palm trees camels
a cautious rug merchant   one hand
on the tent, face turned toward the horizon
turning back like Thomas Jefferson
towards his black *anima*, like Lot's wife
or the thousands of black women
who fled slavery preferring instead
the monastic beds of the River Niger

it is said those waters flowed
red for years
shades of ochre fuchsia and russet
as layers of blood sifted
through the silt of the river
the velvet sands on that tapestry
were red and flowed into all corners
my aunts sat in a line beneath this scene
refusing to turn back
wagging their heads against the world's sins

I have seen more than my aunts dared to see
how each Sunday they sat bare assed and defiant

their dark female caverns linking thighs
into matching hills of lemon ebony and mocha flesh
how the wooden humps reflected off my grandmother's
whalebone hairpins when she leaned into the light
the crumbling walls of the city of Benin
Kamahameha's feathered cape in the Bishop museum

I have seen Buenos Aires
where ladies dine inside their mirrors
Berlin where my blackness
was examined in six languages
Bogotá where there are no traffic signals
and even pregnant women are targets
fat clumsy figures playing toreador
with foreign made limousines

in the Middle East fairy chimneys
of volcanic tuffs spiral into the sunlight
their colors glowing like stained glass
in the half light of the desert
shades of ochre russet and ebony
thrust into tidal waves of magma
and firestorm of ash
like beads on a rosary linking
village to village

when I was eight my prudish aunts
sat like squat pigeons on the horsehair sofa
brazen under their stiff collared dresses
and I gathered dreams of love
from a tapestry woven in velvet
a blood colored crescent moon, three palm trees
two burgundy camels, all arched around
a shadowy figure entering a tent
the world behind him barren and flat

some days pressed by the low ceiling
of a troubled sky I drift back to that room
the scene spreads before me
the delicate red tracery
of some ancient artisan
clinging to thread bare spots
the nomad who is forever coming home
the tent with its doorway of secrets
the dark face turned toward the corner
staring at some fixed point
on the amber horizon of that velvet desert
as if to say how vast
and naked the world seems to be

"TAPESTRIES" IS A POEM ABOUT WOMEN, MORE PRECISELY, ABOUT THE WOMEN ON MY MOTHER'S side of the family. My grandmother gave birth to almost a score of girls and only one boy, so I grew up in this family of women and it was only natural that a great deal of my writing has been directly influenced by them. My most vivid memories of those women comes from a time when my mother and I lived with my grandmother. That was during the '40s, a time when the world was at war, and the men in my family, like most of the other neighborhood men, were serving in the military. I was surrounded by women. Every week they would gather at my grandmother's house and dissect the world along the lines of love and war, birth and death, loyalty and treachery. Most of my early poems about family grew out of those meetings, but by the time "Tapestries" began to take shape, I almost had convinced myself that I'd plumbed all my family memories. Then, in an antique shop on the West Coast, I saw a tapestry, a 1920s rendition of a desert scene done in a beige monochrome of palm trees, camels, and impossibly stylized Arabs. It was all too familiar. My grandmother's parlor had held a similar tapestry, and the frayed threads of the antique store tapestry triggered the memory of that room and the weekly visits of her daughters.

The times I remember the most vividly were summers, perhaps because during the winter, school kept me too busy to find time doing what I liked best, eavesdropping when my mother's sisters came to visit us. Summers in St. Louis are humid, and in my grandmother's house, that humidity made the urgency of their conversations even more pressing. It was a slot of a house, no wider than one room and the adjacent hallway, but running several rooms in length like a railroad sleeping car. Rooms banked off the long dim hallway, dark even at the height of the day. We lived on the second floor and the parlor was the first door at the top of the stairs. In the summer, the heat crept up the stairs as soon as the front door opened, and women spent most of the time fanning themselves as they drank glasses of Kool-Aid and chewed on the weight of the world. And because it was so hot, they dressed the way many southern women dressed to keep themselves cool and free of heat rash: in loose skirts, open front blouses, and little or no underwear. I remember them sitting in the dim light of the parlor, fanning away the heat of the day, and on the wall behind them, a desert scene of camels waiting under a cluster of palm trees while someone leaving—or entering—a tent turned back for a moment as if to see who was doing all that talking. That tapestry seemed to add to the heat of the room.

I know that I did not understand all that was said, because while the scene itself seems clear their conversations are a muddle of phrases and warnings. I know now that the room presented some measure of safety to us at a time when the world was in chaos. The women talked about the war, food rationing, men who'd fled the draft, and women who were spending too much time cheering up the soldiers on leave. And I crouched under my grandmother's rosewood table, half listening while the desert scene maintained its own posture of intrigue. And under that tapestry, my sense of the outside world, with its pitfalls and temptations, began to take shape. Somewhere in there, I was lured toward the outside world as surely as the figure in the tapestry was tempted to look back at the vast desert stretching away from the tent.

There is a well-known adage that says a writer has but one story to tell and tells it again and again. I have never quite believed that to be true, but if that is the case, then "Tapestries" is close to the center of the story that compels me to write. In the case of "Tapestries," *compel* is the most appropriate word I could choose to describe how I came to write that poem, for how else can I explain my compulsion to reveal what I had almost come to regard as sacred: unveiling family secrets I'd eavesdropped on while my mother's sisters gossiped. And more damaging yet, hinging the poem on the absence of [*gasp*] underwear when these women gathered in my grandmother's shoebox of a house in the stifling humidity of St. Louis summer afternoons. This poem, for me, was full of taboos but I could not let go of it; indeed, part of me did not want the poem to be finished. When I first submitted it to the publisher of *Lie And Say You Love Me*, I did so apologetically. How could I have revealed such an intimate part of my family's history? I asked myself. And even more, Who would want to read about such? But this poem clearly mirrors my obsession with a time when the world was the space of one room, my grandmother and her daughters grounding me to a horizon that has forever shaped my life. Since those days, I have traveled to almost all of the world's continents, and yet, like that nomad, home remains intriguing despite all of the mysteries I have encountered.

Thomas McGrath

Ars Poetica:
Or: Who Lives in the Ivory Tower?

Perhaps you'd like a marching song for the embattled prolet-
Ariat, or a realistic novel, the hopeful poet
Said, or a slice of actual life with the hot red heart's blood running,
The simple tale of a working stiff, but better than Jack London?

Nobody wants your roundelay, nobody wants your sestina,
Said the housewife, we want Hedy Lamarr and Gable at the cinema,
Get out of my technicolor dream with your tragic view and your verses;
Down with iambic pentameter and hurray for Louella Parsons.

Of course you're free to write as you please, the liberal editor answered,
But take the red flags out of your poem—we mustn't offend the censor—
And change this stanza to mean the reverse, and you must tone down this
     passage;
Thank God for the freedom of the press and a poem with a message!

Life is lousy enough without you should put it into a sonnet,
Said the man in the street, so keep it out of the novel, the poem, the drama;
Give us a paean of murder and rape, or the lay of a willing maiden,
And to hell with the Bard of Avalon and to hell with Eliot Auden.

Recite the damn things all day long, get drunk on smoke come Sunday,
I respect your profession as much as my own, but it don't pay off when
     you're hungry;
You'll have to carry the banner instead—said the hobo in the jungle—
If you want to eat; and don't forget: it's my bridge you're sleeping under.

Oh it's down with art and down with life and give us another reefer—
They all said—give us a South Sea isle, where light my love lies dreaming;
And who is that poet come in off the streets with a look unleal and lour?
Your feet are muddy, you son-of-a-bitch, get out of our ivory tower.

The Tactical and the Strategic

THOMAS McGRATH WROTE HIS "ARS POETICA" SOMETIME DURING 1947, AND FIRST PUBLISHED
it among the poems of *Longshot O'Leary's Garland of Practical Poesie* (International
Publishers, 1949). During the late Thirties, McGrath had gone to school on the poetry of
Berthold Brecht. He admired Brecht's courageous, straight-forward approach in a kind of
poem he came to call "tactical" as opposed to "strategic" poetry. The tactical poem appeals
directly to the reader's will; the strategic poem is more "consciousness-expanding."
McGrath offers 18th and 19th century Methodist hymns as prototypes. The tactical poem

assumes a *feeling* is already there: it assumes no need to instill a fresh spirit, but to energize, to heighten a pre-existing sensibility. "Ars Poetica" is exemplary McGrath modeled on the Brechtian original.

Born in the Midwest in 1916, the son of a Wobbly, McGrath was a Rhodes Scholar whose time at Oxford was postponed by World War II and a stint in the Aleutian Islands. A blue-collar socialist among the Oxford dons, his art and life were made of just such seeming contradictions. After the war, the American people wanted to escape from thoughts of war. They wanted homecomings and movies and a return to a quieter life. Returning from Oxford, the poet faced the beginning of the McCarthy Era, red-baiting, the Cold War ethic that would eventually lead to his own appearance on the blacklists.

His poems didn't appear in the *Partisan Review* or other "liberal" journals. He didn't belong to any literary movements that issued manifestoes. His manifestoes were his poems. He knew the traditions of English verse from Beowolf to Bunting and Hugh MacDiarmid. Among the poets of mid-century, perhaps only Hayden Carruth approaches McGrath for technical virtuosity and sheer variety. Interior, exterior, slant, and implied rhyme; metrical and non-metrical measures, open forms, haiku-like epigrams; the great epic *Letter to an Imaginary-Friend*; ballads, lyrics, blues—Thomas McGrath wrote all kinds of poetry in all kinds of ways, including tactical and strategic. And he wrote them from the center of his heart.

"Ars Poetica" showcases his great love of language, his expansive vocabulary and ironic sense of humor, his charm, wit, and caustic view of life in these United States. But most of all, it typifies his incomparable *joie de vivre*. Nonetheless, behind the dynamics of the poem, behind all the satirical good humor and ear for living speech and magnificent replication of themes and events of its time, there is a real essay here on the art of poetry.

by Sam Hamill

What He Thought
for Fabbio Doplicher

We were supposed to do a job in Italy
and, full of our feeling for
ourselves (our sense of being
Poets from America) we went
from Rome to Fano, met
the mayor, mulled
a couple matters over (what's
cheap date, they asked us; what's
flat drink). Among Italian literati

we could recognize our counterparts:
the academic, the apologist,
the arrogant, the amorous,
the brazen and the glib—and there was one

administrator (the conservative), in suit
of regulation gray, who like a good tour guide
with measured pace and uninflected tone narrated
sights and histories the hired van hauled us past.
Of all, he was most politic and least poetic,
so it seemed. Our last few days in Rome
(when all but three of the New World Bards had flown)
I found a book of poems this
unprepossessing one had written: it was there
in the *pensione* room (a room he'd recommended)
where it must have been abandoned by
the German visitor (was there a bus of *them*?)
to whom he had inscribed and dated it a month before.
I couldn't read Italian, either, so I put the book
back into the wardrobe's dark. We last Americans

were due to leave tomorrow. For our parting evening then
our host chose something in a family restaurant, and there
we sat and chatted, sat and chewed,
till, sensible it was our last
big chance to be poetic, make
our mark, one of us asked
                        "What's poetry?
Is it the fruits and vegetables and
marketplace of Campo dei Fiori, or
the statue there?" Because I was

the glib one, I identified the answer
instantly, I didn't have to think—"The truth
is both, it's both," I blurted out. But that
was easy. That was easiest to say. What followed
taught me something about difficulty,
for our underestimated host spoke out,
all of a sudden, with a rising passion, and he said:

The statue represents Giordano Bruno,
brought to be burned in the public square
because of his offense against
authority, which is to say
the Church. His crime was his belief
the universe does not revolve around
the human being: God is no
fixed point or central government, but rather is
poured in waves through all things. All things
move. "If God is not the soul itself, He is
the soul of the soul of the world." Such was
his heresy. The day they brought him
forth to die, they feared he might
incite the crowd (the man was famous
for his eloquence). And so his captors
placed upon his face
an iron mask, in which

he could not speak. That's
how they burned him. That is how
he died: without a word, in front
of everyone.
         And poetry—
                  (we'd all
put down our forks by now, to listen to
the man in gray; he went on
softly)—
         poetry is what

he thought, but did not say.

BECKETT SAYS TEARS ARE LIQUIFIED BRAIN. POEMS HAD BETTER COME FROM THAT SAME PLACE.
Beckett knew very well how to laugh, but the laugh had last gasps in it. One writes poems
as one lives, with full attention to the partiality of things.

Lynne McMahon

Toward Eve
from "In The Garden"

Up the cement steps and cracked
Sidewalk with its hairline of grass, up
The wood ramp to the porch which is
Beginning a slow sag and rotting
Just perceptibly in the crosshatch
Of latched sticks on the underside,
Off in the shadiest corner contracted
Against the light—this
Is where you kneel. This is the first
Morning after the sea's departure,
After the fish spines adding their nitrogen
To the loam, after the plankton.
In tiny knuckles of upturning life,
The ferns push up into their brains,
Pushing, straightening, finally one morning
(In the thousand hours of the first
Morning) no longer the green sea horses
Of infant plants. They are astride
The earth now, tall
In their first arrogance. The book
Doesn't say how soon they will bend
To the soil and the hidden nocturnal
Creatures beneath. On that, the book
Is silent, as the ferns are, as the woman
Is who stoops to direct their waters, tending
And blending in, as on the sixth day.

IN THE ACCOUNT GENESIS GIVES US, AFTER THE WORLD AND ADAM ARE BROUGHT INTO BEING, Eve is fashioned, and on the seventh day God rests. What happens on that seventh day? The book doesn't tell us. Creation is complete, presumably, and God is elsewhere, absent. That lacuna interests me; it is, I think, the locus of possibility, the *still-to-come*, though this time in the human dimension. "Toward Eve" is an attempt to come to the brink of poetic creation: we are taken—in slow motion—up the steps of a decrepit porch to a particular corner where we kneel and look at the fern bed beneath. The ferns, ancient and original, have overnight unfurled from their seahorse-shaped infancy into tall, adult plants. They stand straight up for one brief span, then they arc back toward the earth. In terms of the creation myth, they stand before they fall. In this poem, they haven't yet bent; their destiny has not yet been cast; it is still the sixth day. The reader knows they will bend, knows Eve will enter the story to change it forever. But at this moment, everything is silent, and the woman, whose poem this is, stoops to water the plants, still tending and blending in, still part of the Garden on the sixth day.

The poem is an ars poetica not so much in its intention, which may be oblique, but in its method. Before the writing of the poem, the gathering of materials. Before the comprehension, the observation. And therefore the attention paid as minutely as possible to the surrounds of the poem—the cracked sidewalk with its hairline of grass, the rot beginning in the crosshatch of latched sticks, the tiny knuckles of infant ferns. The accuracy of observation is the first step, for without that, no resolution, no "creation" is possible. Eve tends and blends in, yes, but she is also taking in the garden, preparing the ground for her own creation. She is about to depart from the script, and what she does on that seventh day is not recorded. Perhaps she begins to daydream, to imagine a serpent. Genesis doesn't say. The book only records the raw material of the world; what Eve makes of it, or the poet, comes later.

Sandra McPherson

Two Men Trading Dance Movements at Tabby's Blues Box and Heritage Hall, Baton Rouge

Whatever is expressive
about clumsiness (bad knees),
   disproportion (potbelly,
putto hands), untaught
   self-portraiture,
wall-hugging, cold
   feet, or stillness—
chilled into models—
   painters must jar
to life,
     we may like this
   more, seeing
how these men start from an uncandescent
   corner by the entry door
(not at the back
   by the restrooms'
mussed, rampageous
   tulip colors)
and match up: two men,
   simply, by image,
but impulse-different, nerve-distinct.

And so, beginning from this vertex,
   the two
open like radiolarians—
   one with blazing glass bones
raving from its nucleus,
   the other living out
of an invisible core
   with a burst
of tines (like burrs,
   chinquapin nuts, globefish)
at the globe-surface (wands,
   extrusions, rep of
waffles and honeycombs, cages
   permuting to regalia,
those microscopic bombastic
   laces, cacti, and grilles,
the bizarre—a hairnet over antlers,

javelins
beside featherstitching), and
    alternate astonishing
each other with outward-firing
    or inward-brawling flurries
of their two repertoires, one
    a medusa disentangling,
the other formal as a Caspian tern.

One morning, later, after
    a downpour, I track raindrops
where hairs on a flume-creased tree-lupine leaf
    roll them into spheres,
and under a hand lens see dancers,
    magnifying partners,
bump the diving-bell edge,
    a tense bay window,
and propel there, a pair
    in a room not yet evaporated.
These two
    are in a tournament
and I recall
    how one man, pearl-three-pieced
and cubist, dances his
    points, lines, angles,
surfaces, and solids,
    then the other,
in work blues, purling,
    water-snaky, suddenly
up through the waist sends a shudder
    into shoulders, forearms, hands over head
to traverse the room
    in a turbidity whipping up something
like the gasp
    at Jules Lion's first New Orleans
daguerreotypes that there is a whole
    re-erected city there
yet every detail—an insect
    on a stone of a cathedral—
can be discerned, lucid in itself.

What esteem
    they are paying each other,
stretching a flat hand out
    to the other's palm, back
and forth all evening until the elegant
    man decides the serpentine
has won, concedes but is so pleased
    he holds the other's grip a moment.
These are not dances
    the world knows; they are inside
explosions, privity,
    idiosyncrasy with
molecularly fine technique.
    When paint peels
off Tabby's walls, when the photographs
    of road-brumous singers
curl around their tacks,
    that is how they move,
this is contractual art,
    fleshed fireworks, a making
for the other
    of a signal pointing
away from isolation,
    a countersign that will only work if
aurified by *horror vacui*
    and tavern lamp
and encountered
    round a corner,
a prospect contracting them to be—
    with acutest scope—
infinitesimally
    visible together,
down to
    the winner's work keys
still ringed
    to his belt loop.

Air

Naturally it is night.
Under the overturned lute with its
One string I am going my way
Which has a strange sound.

This way the dust, that way the dust.
I listen to both sides
But I keep right on.
I remember the leaves sitting in judgment
And then winter.

I remember the rain with its bundle of roads.
The rain taking all its roads.
Nowhere.

Young as I am, old as I am,

I forget tomorrow, the blind man.
I forget the life among the buried windows.
The eyes in the curtains.
The wall
Growing through the immortelles.
I forget silence
The owner of the smile.

This must be what I wanted to be doing,
Walking at night between the two deserts,
Singing.

Carol Muske

To the Muse
New Year's Eve, 1990

She danced topless, the light-eyed drunken girl
who got up on the bow of our pleasure boat
last summer in the pretty French Mediterranean.

Above us rose the great grey starboard flank
of an aircraft carrier. Sailors clustered
on the deck above, cheering, and the caps rained down,

a storm of insignia: *S.S. Eisenhower.*
I keep seeing the girl when I tell you
the Eisenhower's now in the Gulf, as if

the two are linked: the bare-breasted dancer
and a war about to be fought over oil. Caps fell
on the bow and she plucked one up, set it rakishly

on her red hair. In the introspective manner
of the very drunk, she tipped her face dreamily up,
wet her lips, an odalisque, her arms crossed akimbo

on the cap. Someone, a family member, threw a shirt
over her and she shrugged it off, laughing, palms
fluttering about her nipples. I tell you I barely knew

those people, but you, you liked the girl, you
liked the ship. You liked to fuck, you told me.
The sex of politics is its intimate divisive plural,

we, us, ours. *Who's over there?* you ask—*not us.*
Your pal is there, a flier stationed on a carrier.
He drops the jet shrieking on the deck. Pitch dark:

he lowers the nose toward a floating strip of
lit ditto marks and descends. Like writing haiku—
the narrator is a landscape. A way of staying subjective

but humbling the perceiver: a pilot's view.
When you write to your friend I guess that
there are no margins, you want him to see

everything you see and so transparent is
your kind bravado: he sees that too. Maybe
he second-guesses your own desire to soar over

the sand ruins, sit yourself in the masked pit
and rise fifteen hundred screaming feet a minute
into an inaccessible shape: falcon, hawk—Issa's

blown petals? Reinvent war, then the woman's faithless
enslaved dance. Reinvent sailors bawling at the rail
and the hail of cliches: flash of legs on the slave deck.

Break the spell, reverse it: caps on the waves as they
toss away their uniforms, medals, stars. Then the girl
will wake up, face west, a lengthening powerful figurehead

swept gold with fire. The waves keep coming: the you, the me,
the wars. Here is the worst of it, stripped, humiliated—
or dancing on the high deck, bully-faced, insatiable.

Here is the lie that loves us as history personified,
here's the personification: muse, odalisque, soldier,
nightfall—swear to us—this time, you will make it right.

War and the warrior, as historical themes, are linked in my mind to images of women dancing, not as emblems of the eroticization of conflict, but as Robert Hass says in his great poem "The Origin of Cities," a figure *for action simply. She dances,* he says, *the ships go forth.* This is not to deny all the other war-symbol figures: Helen, Penelope and their sisters—war brides, Mata Haris, as well as the traditional chaste guardians of the hearth. But the female figure dances through history as act, a step in the initiation of the warrior and of trade, *a figure of the outward,* a send-off. These were some of the thoughts I had in mind as "To the Muse" began to form itself.

As the threat of the Persian Gulf War became a reality around New Year's Eve 1990, I found myself "re-seeing" an afternoon I'd spent with my husband and eight-year-old daughter on a business associate's boat in the Mediterranean off Cap d'Antibes the summer before. It was a bright hot day, the water was a deep cobalt blue, we pulled up to a floating bar near a rocky reef serving cold drinks and citron glacés. It was lovely, but we felt uneasy, we didn't know these people well, we had other places to go, and although the thought of a sybaritic afternoon, sunning and buzzing about on the blue water was tempting, we were eager to get back to shore. Nevertheless, our host had more to show us: speeding ahead, he piloted his boat close to the huge looming flank of an aircraft carrier, the U.S.S. Eisenhower. We gazed up at the sailors, who waved good-naturedly at us from the high deck. Suddenly, our host's twenty-something daughter, a little tipsy, announced that she craved a sailor's cap emblazoned with the S.S. Eisenhower insignia. The "tradeoff" was a demi-striptease, she said. She proceeded to dance on the deck of our boat, bare-breasted, as caps (and cheers) came raining down.

Months later, back in L.A., when I heard the announcement that the Eisenhower had left the Mediterranean and was proceeding to the Gulf, I thought of that afternoon, our embarrassment, the young woman's drunkenness and abandon, the cheering sailors. What was embarrassing was how she was so quickly reduced to a symbol of commerce. She wasn't a particularly beautiful woman,—but that's not why there was no beauty in her actions. Neither was there mystery or grace in her dancing, just *negotiation,* she was working to get something.

This poem speculates on the evolution of the act, the dance: this conceit-turned-commerce, the "tradeoffs" of war, the woman's role as erotic "figurehead" on prow and screen. How we keep striking the same old bargain, falling for the same old tricks in war and the wars of love. The poem wants to extend this inquiry to the notion of the Muse, first as general inspiration, then a more personal take. There's a guy I know, a good friend, whose buddy was a flier in the Gulf and we'd had an argument about the war. This guy and my dialogue with him, are at the heart of the poem. I try to imagine his feeling, so different from my own—and how war is "reinvented" through feelings like his, which are persuasive because they are, or seem to be, "history" personified. I try to take each archetypal "lie" history tells us: the dancing girl, the sailor, the Muse, the warrior and the lover and follow each to its ironic end: *let me be transformed one more time, let me be heroic.*

In that sense, the poem seems cynical—but really it's quite boneheadedly idealistic—I actually talk about "breaking the spell" at one point, reversing, or re-ordering it, changing history. The "haiku-view" of history, where the narrator is a landscape, subjective but humble, belongs (sadly) only to pilots. The poem itself suffers, I think, from a rather overly-insistent point-of-view, but that's another issue. Questions of style in this poem must inevitably be secondary to tone, because the credibility of the voice in this long apostrophe-cum-dialogue is everything here. In that sense, I'm just another cliche of history, the poet with the point-of-view.

Pulling in the Nets
— Lake Cachuma, California

The wheat cock up their shoulders and turn away
                                                from a confidential breeze.
But along the road side they might bend low in their stalks,
                                                face down in straightjackets.
It's hard to duck the sickle with such delicate spines.

I saw a whitish bird buckle
across the window of a motor home.
                                One quick pop of the neck
and flutter-whirl of chest down
                                to dislodge its soul—
heavy beyond the millions of insects
flaked from the grill.

                        *   *   *

Fettered saplings around the tract homes of Camarillo
yield up their thin boughs, shake them in the wind
as if in hope of retreat
                                down through their lashings
where spring, though blue across the plains,
                                        stays somnolent
in the cracks of white dirt
                        which zag the flowerbed.

In Santa Barbara there's not much difference.
Tense layers of jacaranda buds
                                snap under cyclists
and give their small sighs back to the wasp
                                        and the hornet. . . .
Here, in the muddy reservoir
                        spiked with ghost limbs
the spillway is clogged
                        with autumn's net—
the buoys float unattended
                        with the dingy foam.

                        *   *   *

I'm guilty of the silk dust of butterfly wings
                                resilient on my fingers.
Legs spasmed and tucked hopelessly.
                                If it was penance,
it was an awful one, but even the monarch

with its high-ranking brassard
                                        takes to the wind like litter.
No one suffers for that. . . .

I can't be blamed. I'm like a pull of fur
on barbed wire rocking gently in this breeze,
wanting nothing more
                                than to float to the grass.
Truth is a salt block which seems to melt itself back.
I am a small tongue
                        which no longer gives
to the spongy tricks of the peach.
                                        And why should I?
If I had the choice,
                and I do,
the pomegranate would be my bucolic
                                with its tiny poems of blood
to gash my chin and spill over my wrist,
staining me beyond the seine of this life—
the pith shredded and sluiced away.

I AM INTERESTED IN THE SPIRITUAL FOREMOST, THE REACH FOR IT THROUGH THE LANGUAGE OF
personal experience. This poem is more imagistic than my newer ones, and it represents
an experiment of charging the associational imagery of the imagination with language
and charging language with the associational imagery of the imagination. It seems to me
very different from what I'm writing now, which are short narrative poems in a lyric
mode; that is to say, the charge of language is still incredibly important. But I also seem
to be insisting, lately, on the factual personal experience which seems to me the only hon-
est, effective, true way to explore both social and political conditions as well as the sub-
lime and the transcendental.

I suppose the whitish bird, the insects and butterfly refer to a moral order I believed
in or was struggling with when I wrote this poem. And as much as the [un]natural envi-
ronment of the second section might seem to be an indictment to some, it is really more
of a waking dream, and as such it prefigures the subject of later poems of mine—an actu-
al tragic accident, which I had previous to writing this poem, and the issue of responsi-
bility. The experiences of this poem are not directly related to the accident, but they are
all true, factual, held in uncertainty within the mind with a faith in the poetic activity
and as a testament to the indelible nature of the poetic activity in an individual's life.

Walter Pavlich

Stan Laurel Tutors a Would-Be Comedian

If the scene calls
for surprise

pretend the last
chocolate in the box

is hollow
and you eat into

a bee. Then
blink

like brassy wings.
The exag-

gerators chew
wasps

or put a hornet
in their watch-

pocket. Don't
be a smart

Alexander.
Remember rump

humor. Use
your silly buttocks.

Ease down
on a rubber

nail. Taste
your bee.

Poetry, Comedy, Elders

I'VE ALWAYS HAD FRIENDS WHO WERE MUCH OLDER THAN ME. MOST OF THEM ARE WRITERS. Their strengths have always been obvious to me. Their kindness complete. But what I've also appreciated, and learned from, are their admitted fears, hesitations, doubts, serious and not-so-serious concerns. They matched my eagerness to know, an almost obnoxious over-eagerness at times to know, with their patience, experience, and wisdom.

I've witnessed this give and take process in other callings. I've heard the elder blues-man backstage answer every question of a young wannabe. Or demonstrate the quirkiest chord progressions and time changes.

I've watched as a gospel singer (who's sung for decades) takes in new group members and grooms them for life on the road, on the "gospel highway." What clothes to wear, what food to eat, but mainly what to avoid in order to keep his "soul right." So when it's time to put all of their voices together . . .

Roscoe "Fatty" Arbuckle took in Buster Keaton and showed him what could be done on film as opposed to on the stage. Chaplin taught Chaplin and was cagey enough to control the making of almost all of his films. Even to the point of re-shooting certain scenes hundreds of times.

Whenever Oliver Hardy was asked to explain something about comedy, he deferred with this "Ask Stan." Stan Laurel learned his trade in the British music halls and was involved in every aspect of filmmaking when the studios allowed him to be, to the point of watching and editing that day's rushes well into the night. When he lost control over these processes their films deteriorated. Just like Keaton's.

After Oliver Hardy died in 1957, Stan Laurel refused to perform again. He retired with his wife to an apartment overlooking the ocean in Santa Monica. Someone discovered that his name was listed in the phone book. Fans rang his doorbell on a regular basis. Among them were Dick Cavett, Jerry Lewis, Danny Kaye, Peter Sellers . . . I've read where Sellers invoked Stan Laurel's screen character as he created his Chauncey Gardiner in *Being There.*

In my poem I try to distill some of Stan Laurel's views on character and technique. As far as my own ars poetica, *"Ask my poems."*

Lucia Maria Perillo

The Roots of Pessimism in Model Rocketry, The Fallacy of Its Premise

X-Ray had a see-thru payload chamber.
The Flying Saucer model was a gyp—
unless you were the kind of kid who loved
the balsa wood shredding more than airtime,
the smashing down more than the going up.
When Big Bertha sheared my brother's pinkie
I watched medicine make its promise good:
in the future we would all be androids.
The doctors reinstalled his milky nail
and drained blue fingertip, though afterward
I felt a little cheated. Already
I'd envisioned how his mutant terrors
could be put to my use, the naked stub
unsheathed to jinx an enemy sneaker.

We were a tribe of Josef Mengeles
doing frontier science: putting crickets
in the payload, betting if they'd return
alive or dead. I always bet on death
because they always came down dead, I was
the pessimist, the child of many coins.
When someone fished from the dusty ballfield
the cocktail sausage of my brother's loss,
I gave its odds less than even money.
My vote was Put the finger in a can,
send it to Estes Model Rocket Co.
who would feel guilty enough to send cash.
But guilt turned on me. Now my brother's hand
looks perfect, except when he makes a fist.

THESE DAYS WHEN THE POETIC COMMUNITY THREATENS TO IMPLODE ON ITSELF, WHEN POETRY'S only readers are said to be its writers, many poets (myself included) have shied away from writing poems about poetry. If we hope to gain a larger readership, it seems logical that our poems should come from the realm of common experience—work or love or family, for example, and not from the hermetic experience of wrangling with words. Even Czeslaw Milosz, author of the most often-cited ars poetica of our current literature, puts a question mark after that term when he takes it for the title of his poem, which ends up declaring itself an exercise in self-defeat.

I wrote "The Roots of Pessimism . . ." in response to years of having my poems described as "dark," "brutal" and "grim." Though the poem had its beginnings as an exploration of my own poetic habits, I was pleased when "poetry" found a way to gracefully exit the poem, which was left standing on its one allegorical leg. Rockets, as things that honor a reality beyond words, are more interesting than poems anyway.

I know it is critically fashionable to believe that language precedes or obliterates this reality, but those of us who are newcomers—who have spent more time outside the poetic community than as rubber-stamped insiders—will be damned if we're to abandon the real world after struggling so long to figure out how to speak of it. That's why I think the best ars poeticas will always support a dual reading: they will be poems that tell us not only how to send decent poems into the world, but also how to send ourselves into that same world as decent men and women.

Consenting

In your best dream, everything responds
and smiles with the loving awkwardness,
the sudden, blurred readjustments of
a group photograph. There is a word
for everyone. There is a sky
filled with the tops of trees and letters
hanging from them, spelling your name.

All the answers you can accept
begin there. Rooted, like ideal
children, in that locale where answers
are things you touch, they wear the features
of a world too easy to fail
or be struck dumb. They sing to themselves.
They cheerfully explain that gardens

flourish without you, that the tall,
bright windows that look onto gardens
shine because there is no one in them.
A comfort, an accounting for absence
signed with your own name. You can
walk out into the afternoon's
exact center and disappear,

knowing, now, that what becomes
of you has a place reserved among all
the words and smiles you have arranged
in your best dream. Which is to say
that the world loves you back and is changed
permanently by what you do.
As simple as that. To want some things to live

because they will live anyway,
to look at a photograph
of strangers waving up to you
from a garden somewhere in New Haven,
makes your share of the world possible.
It adds a name to the list. It fills
the sky with the tops of trees and letters.

AN ARS POETICA MUST OFTEN BE AN ACCIDENTAL OCCASION, AN INADVERTENT TESTIMONY, IF
only because a poem's meaning is the effect and not the cause of composition. I wrote
"Consenting" in a hotel room in Hartford, having spent the preceding day sitting in a car
parked outside of Wallace Stevens' house. The poem was an act of resistance to my own
fascination with that house, with the poems that emerged from it, with the florid ciphers
that seemed to garland the air surrounding it. And in resistance, I found one gesture of
what I mean to say.

Alberto Ríos

Teodoro Luna's Two Kisses

Mr. Teodoro Luna in his later years had taken to kissing
His wife
Not so much with his lips as with his brows.
This is not to say he put his forehead
Against her mouth—
Rather, he would lift his eyebrows, once, quickly:
Not so vigorously he might be confused with the villain
Famous in the theaters, but not so little as to be thought
A slight movement, one of accident. This way
He kissed her
Often and quietly, across tables and through doorways,
Sometimes in photographs, and so through the years themselves.
This was his passion, that only she might see. The chance
He might feel some movement on her lips
Toward laughter.

The Language I Write In

WHEN I WAS THREE OR FOUR, MY PARENTS BOUGHT A NEW HOUSE IN WHAT WOULD LATER become a small suburb of Nogales, Arizona, on the border of Mexico, some four miles outside town. My father was born in Mexico, on the border of Guatemala, and my mother was born in England. I had languages.

As we kept driving out to watch the house being built, my mother got to make a number of choices regarding details, among which was the color of various rooms.

My mother, when asked what color she wanted the kitchen, said to the workers who were all Mexican, and who spoke very little English, *limón*. She said it both because she wanted the kitchen to be yellow and because she wanted to start learning Spanish. The workers nodded yes. But when we came back the next day, the kitchen was painted bright green, like a small jungle. Mexican *limones*, my mother found out, are small and green, that color exactly, no mistake.

So that's the color the wall stayed for the next eight years. She said it was a reminder to us all that there was a great deal to learn in the world. You might laugh at first, but after eight years you start to think about it.

And she was right. It was a perfect, small example of that other way to see things, and for eight years the kitchen for us was, perhaps in a very large way, an even better place than school.

*   *   *

I had languages, but my first language was the language of listening. Maybe it was the language of seeing. Figuring that out took me a long time. I get in, and get put in, the middle of debates on things like bilingualism, and I get asked questions about whether I write in English or Spanish, or both. Somewhere along the line English and Spanish got all the billing. But it occurs to me that I write in the language of listening.

I look for it, I smell for it, wherever it is. I follow it. I used to look for language in words, rather than things, even though I knew better. When I was young, I talked to my grandmother this way: she would cook, and I would eat. The whole exchange was not about words at all, but it's how we talked best.

This language is about more than recognizing something from both sides. It's about first recognizing something inside of all the words for it. The more I learn about language, the more I don't know which one is mine. What I do know is that I am constantly on the lookout for more of it, for those places in language that actually speak.

I think of this writing as a movement. I think of myself moving laterally *through* things, not in a linear way *toward* them. I move sideways and I stay with the moment. There's more than mere beginning and ending in that. This is what "Teodoro Luna's Two Kisses" does; it is more than kissing; it's what kissing is, for the moment and through the years. On its own terms and in its own language. This is how it came to me, and how I give it back.

And Continuing

In his eyes & hands a brash assurance, delight
masked as a boast, even when he knows his life adjudged
by force
and denials. This is the Max Beckman Max Beckman
painted in his mid-30's. And if the mirror no longer leans,
wedged between a doll house & chiffonnier,
in some Bremerhaven attic,
if it's smashed & exists now only as dust motes
that invade a circle of lamp light or alter
a North Sea sunset? Well, he could never be broken,
or dispersed. Confronted in black
evening tux, his face thickening, a smile
aware of its vanities. Hair the color of gravity trapped
between a hammer & anvil. In his right hand,
half-smoked, a cigar. The curl of smoke
invisible. Insouciance,
amused, & protected by the complete
lack of insouciance that is self-knowledge.
The left hand held away from the jacket,
shooing something off,
palm out, so his wrist shows—
the skin there soft, & embarrassed, by rosiness,
pulsing slightly,
like this woman's neck, as she stands with me waiting
for the traffic signal. Its curve to her collarbone
the place on a body where I love to think
the world begins, there between two or three freckles.
All the world. Starting from this street corner,
an Isuzu jeep idling, garter belt
tied to its rear-view, & by the cable TV truck
two kids in maroon soccer togs, the crossing guard loafing,
starting with them. Spreading
to include the violence of a summer evening, the MDC pools,
the rib joints, & talk of software licensing
near the horse rider, the bronze
mediocrity of the horse's withers, & past
the paddle boats & kick boxers in the park,
out beyond them, to fields,
snapdragons, golden rod, interstates, foxglove,
spreading out like foxglove. And starting here
I promise my pleasure to be so large to be right
even if eventually doomed.

PERHAPS I HAVE ALWAYS BEEN ONE OF THOSE PEOPLE WITH A BAD HABIT OF AUTOMATIC HOPE-lessness, of being all too ready to sign up to sail the doomish seas, and so, as to be convinced of being glad to be alive, I have had to be educated by burning embers and falling I-beams, by arson and wreckage. Fortunately, I've had other teachers, and Max Beckman was one of these. Beckman's paintings own the sense of "serious play," of doom *and* possibility, I have always felt in the poets I love best—Vallejo, Berryman, Akhmatova, W. C. Williams, Levine, among others. "And Continuing" started out less as an homage than as an attempt to describe to myself the complete lack of illusions, combined with amused faithfulness, that I felt in Beckman's great *Self-Portrait*, which hangs now in the Fogg Museum just around the corner from my house. I might as well have tried describing the genetic engineering of an Asiatic lily. Somewhere along the line, the poem became a note of instruction to myself: about how, like Beckman's paintings, I wanted my own work always to turn toward the world and the people who live in it, how I ought to be willing to pay the price (as Beckman did in many ways), and how it is possible to be homeless and still find a home.

Len Roberts

Shoveling while the Snow Keeps Falling

How many times have I found myself
out here shoveling while the flakes
   keep falling, the low rumble
of my voice like that of the shovel
as it scrapes the pitted concrete,
my wife's words in my ears, Why
go out while it's still snowing? I
can't tell her my father comes back
when it snows like this, his brown
   collar up,
the flakes caught in his big wave of
   hair
where they slowly crumple and melt.
That he walks down close to the house
   at night, bows
through the spruce, knocks clumps
of snow from branches in small, explosive
   puffs.
I used to think he wanted to talk
   about
his wife, my mother, the day she left
and he stood by the canal fence and wept,
   but instead
he whispers the shine of the '52 Buick,
tells me he lit candles on St. Bernard's
   altar,
then asks the names of the presidents again,
says the next time he comes he'll expect
me to know the states and their capitals,
   the ones
I've been repeating the past thirty years
   of my life.
When he squats and makes drawings I can't
   see clearly in the snow
he tells me he knows I've been screwing up,
   but it's all
right, he can tell I'm learning to open
   myself

despite the fearful dreams my mother still
    breathes
into my head of my wife leaving with another
    man,
of my sons and daughters being hit by a
    speeding car.
It's not easy, he sighs, waving his hands
in the blueblack air as though they were wind,
telling me as I straighten my back
that I cannot afford to stop and talk,
just keep shoveling no matter
how cold my toes get, no matter
how many times the snow covers
    the clear walk.

THE MAIN POINT OF THIS POEM, AS IT IS WITH MUCH OF MY WRITING, IS THAT I'M OUTSIDE, concentrating, bearing down in some way, doing some work, when the immediate or distant past comes to the fore to be reckoned with—in this poem, it is my father. In the first place, of course, I'm out there so this re-living can take place on a physical as well as an imaginary level; I'm breathing the same cold air I breathed with my father forty years ago, upstate New York, smelling the same pines, seeing the same blue-black cold. The image, then, is a conduit, a connector between the past and present, for the world remains basically the same. And I can finally hear myself (and others) out there clearly, without distortion. So I can talk with my dead, with angels, maybe even God. But, as the poem shows, the visitors don't always tell me what I expect or want to hear, and, as anyone who writes a poem knows, that's the pleasure of listening. If I expect sadness, the message is quite often joy, and vice versa. The past does merge with the present, though, the dead do live again (and I become one of the dead?), and I can talk back, whether it be in the form of reciting the states and their capitals or blurting out my hopes, my fears.

What I hear is the rumble of the shovel as well as my dead father sighing (is it the wind?), telling me that I cannot afford to stop and talk, that there is work to be done. Thus my long, run-on sentences, sometimes a poem consisting of just one sentence that cannot stop. I feel the same urgency to tumble through the poem—the "tumbling," I hope, re-created partially by some severe enjambments as well as the various indented lines—as I do to go out there and shovel the walk. Once I've started, I can't stop (as my father says, "just keep shoveling.") Work and more work. To go out and lift the fallen snow, to hear the voices, write the poems, regardless of the fact that snow will definitely cover it all up again. What could be more life-giving, exhilarating?

And Language Can't Find Me

There are moments when I get distracted in a word I was about to say. Form and sound never quite making it to my throat, image or symbol never becoming a clear thought, the only real sense is an impulse. Like a drug without the drug. Only a man who stands in front of me, inches of space between us. His eyes are waiting for my response.

My response. I need to recall the request. He said something, maybe important, but my body didn't hear. His eyes are looking into mine. He is looking for the lost word. I cannot turn away. I want to cut across all the inches of space between us, amused by my own distortion of distance. Language is stuck on an impulse quivering in my jugular.

There is this fear of falling if he lets go the gaze I am holding onto. I am looking for my voice in his throat and find fear locked under the trachea. He is leaning on the gaze between us like a bridge. This is a balancing act, if either one of us gives into the fear we will fall. I wonder how deep I can fall. This moment is not about hitting bottom but more about getting lost for a split second.

And language can't find me.

Ars Poetica – *Un Tripazo*

THE POEM EXISTS, IS A *TRIP* AS WE WOULD HAVE SAID TWENTY-FIVE YEARS AGO. A TRIP, *UN tripazo*—Chicana translation: Chicanoized term for trip as in the '60s. Word derived from: Chicanoized version of trip; or from *tripa* meaning intestine or gut, to mean from the gut, or gut-level. What a trip. *Que tripazo.*

The process is a trip. It begins with the brain picking up the impulse, impulse being a strange gnawing at the gut. The words do not exist. Exploration from brain to gut, recalling symbols and language and the merging of the two.

Perhaps.

The language is difficult. The process to find language to arrive at the poem. Bilingual, bicultural, two sets of symbols and two different languages and the total essence of what language embodies. And, that poetry is an art of language and meaning. Poetry means different things in different cultures and is arrived at through different processes and values.

The poem is a trip—*un tripazo.*

¡Orale! Right on! Write on!

Pattiann Rogers

Reaching the Audience
from the introduction to The First Book of Iridaceae

We will start with a single blue dwarf iris
Appearing as a purple dot on a hairstreak
Butterfly seen in a distant pine barrens and proceed
Until we end with a single point of purple spiraling
Like an invisible wing in the center of the flower
Making fact.

We will investigate a stand of blue flags crimsoned
By the last sun still showing over the smoky edges
Of the ravine and illustrate in sequence the glazing
Of those iris by the wet gold of an early dawn.

We will survey a five-mile field of purple iris
Holding bristle-legged insects under the tips
Of their stamens and measure the violet essence
Gathered at the bases of their wings and devote
One section to a molecule of iris fragrance
Preserved and corked in a slender glass.

There will be a composition replicating the motion
Of the iris rolling sun continually over its rills
And another for the stillness of the iris sucking ivory
Moonlight through its hollows making ivory roots.

There will be photographs in series of the eyes
Of a woman studying the sepals of an iris
In a lavender vase and a seven-page account of the crested
Iris burning at midnight in the shape of its flame
And six oriental paintings of purple petals torn apart
And scattered over snow beneath birches and a poem
Tracing a bouquet of blue iris tied together like balloons
Floating across the highest arc of a spring heaven.

There will be an analysis of the word of the iris
In the breath of the dumb and an investigation
Of the touch of the iris in the fingertips of the blind
And a description of the iris-shaped spaces existing
In the forest before the forest became itself
And a delineation of those same blade-thin spaces
Still existing after the forest has been lost again.

It is the sole purpose of these volumes-in-progress
To ensure that anyone stopped anywhere in any perspective
Or anyone caught forever in any crease of time or anyone
Left inside the locked and folded bud of any dream
Will be able to recognize something on these pages
And remember.

Defining the Investigation of Place and Moment

ALTHOUGH THERE ARE SEVERAL POEMS I COULD HAVE CHOSEN TO ADDRESS THE SUBJECT OF MY
ars poetica, for instance, "All the Elements of the Scene," "That Song," "Discovering Your
Subject," "Finding the Tattooed Lady in the Garden," the poem "Reaching the Audience"
seems to me most explicit and complete of them all.

To begin at the ending, the last stanza of this poem states straightforwardly the pur-
pose of "these volumes-in-progress" (the poems forming the body of my work), name-
ly, to try to reach anyone, anywhere, in any situation, with something that will touch and
revive a forgotten memory, to awaken.

The person first touched and awakened is, hopefully, the poet. In order for me to be
enlightened by my poem, I must be wholly present in the work. My body and sensuality
are crucial elements to my writing process. They not only serve as guides to the progres-
sion of the thought in the poem, but they are the only forces to fill and quicken the inert
framework of the language. My body must become the framework of the poem, one with
it, inseparable.

This has most often (but not exclusively) been my tact and approach in my writing:
to investigate a single subject (in the case of this poem, the iris), event or person by
approaching it from all the avenues, angles and perspectives I can imagine, to move
inward and outward and around it, above and below, backward and forward in time,
from the divine to the profane, to treat the subject as thoroughly and completely as I pos-
sibly can and thereby to try to perceive its place in the universe during the moments of
the poem, how its being and presence are determined by its relationships to other enti-
ties, including the poem itself. And I also attempt to examine the subject's effect on the
universe as an actor, not simply a passive recipient of the forces surrounding it. How does
the iris define time and form god?

This goal of my poetry is never fully accomplished, thus the "volumes-in-progress."
But it's a grand game that can be played over and over, if only because every moment of
time adds a new way of viewing an old subject. The iris of five minutes ago is not the iris
of this moment. The poet of five minutes ago is not the poet of this moment. The god of
five minutes ago is not the god of this moment. Is memory of this moment? The task is
never finished.

And, of course, the constant, underlying purpose of poetry toward which I always
aim first is pleasure—joy in the language and its motion, pleasure in the surprise and
turning of thought and perception, happiness in the sound and music of the words,
ebullience in the praise that any act of creation assumes.

I understand my poems as experiments. Language is the tool of the investigation.
The music, craft and techniques of poetry are the skills employed to carry out the inves-
tigation. The results are not static or fixed. They often merely engender a host of new
questions. And the conclusion of the investigation, the finished poem, becomes another
factor itself to be considered in the ongoing process of investigating the universe. This
multiplication of perspective, this expansion and taking-in, this moving out into the vast
and moving back through language is the experience I seek to create again and again.

Mariève Rugo

On Not Being Able to Write

There are icons in memory—
like that first autumn, New York
netting stars in the harsh mesh
of its windows. Or December in Rome,
dawn's cobalt smell after watching
all night death in a brown room.

Or earlier, that garden in Provence,
tangerines in bloom,
the terrace too hot to walk on,
and beyond the white wall,
the flat turquoise bay
where my mother swam naked,
a bronzed fish spattering diamonds.

We create what we remember
to survive all we never had.
In a hall, darkened by exterior glitter,
my father scolds me
for anticipating his gift more than his return.
I am small but I slide an immense distance . . .

as when in a dream, a familiar face slips
off its skull, withers, disappears.

FOR ME, THE ROLE OF MEMORY IS FUNDAMENTAL TO THE PURPOSE OF MY POEMS AS WELL AS TO the creation of their metaphors and imagery. Often the sense of the poem emerges from the collision between how I remember things and how I now understand them to have been.

How I feel about a poem depends almost entirely on how much distance there is between what I had intended and what I find on the page, between memory and apprehended meaning. Frequently, I cannot overcome that distance and have to settle for what I get, which is sometimes more than I'd hoped for. In fact, I've become accustomed to the poem deciding for itself what it wants/needs to say. This is such a poem, in which I began with a series of images from memory and ended with a new understanding. After I comprehended what I was really writing about, it seemed to me that in this poem, the distance between purpose and result is a little smaller than it often is.

I wrote "On Not Being Able to Write" after recovering from a six-year writer's block, a choking silence that still haunts me. One day when I was thinking about what that inability to produce more than scraps and phrases had felt like, a series of images appeared in my mind—images representing moments when what I most needed was taken from me. My arrival in America at ten, knowing from the first instant how alien I was. My mother's death in Rome which left me to cope alone with bitterly unfinished business. The impact of my mother's narcissism and my father's disapproval, dating from my very early childhood (I think I was four that summer in Cannes). Given my present fear of having poetry taken from me again, the connection between images of emotional abandonment and the abandonment of my "muse" seems almost inevitable. At the time the poem was writing itself, I didn't understand why these particular images arrived with this particular title, but feeling the poem's urgency, I managed to stay out of its way so it could say what it seemed determined to say. Now, after countless revisions, I understand what I was writing about and why, and I am, as always, grateful for this strange gift I've been given of explaining my life to myself.

Muriel Rukeyser
To Enter that Rhythm Where the Self is Lost

To enter that rhythm where the self is lost,
where breathing : heartbeat : and the subtle music
of their relation make our dance, and hasten
us to the moment when all things become
magic, another possibility.
That blind moment, midnight, when all sight
begins, and the dance itself is all our breath,
and we ourselves the moment of life and death.
Blinded;   but given now another saving,
the self as vision, at all times perceiving,
all arts all senses being languages,
delivered of will, being transformed in truth—
for life's sake surrendering moment and images,
writing the poem;   in love making;   bringing to birth.

FOR MURIEL RUKEYSER (1913-1980), THE WRITING OF POETRY WAS WHAT SHE CALLED A
dynamic act—a process involving both the artist and the audience. Although the idea might
not seem odd or unfamiliar to us today, it was a radically different way of thinking about
the relationship between reader and writer in the mid-twentieth century when ideas about
the authority of both text and writer were significantly more rigid than they are in our post-
modern, post-structuralist age. The notion of the writing of poetry as a dynamic act was
one that Rukeyser took from science, specifically from her study of the nineteenth-century
founder of physical chemistry, Willard Gibbs, whose life and work she chronicled in a biog-
raphy published in 1942. What she found particularly relevant to her work in poetry were
Gibbs' explorations in systems dynamics and chemical potential. In her thinking about
poetry, Gibbs' depiction of a system as "an agreement of components" became the founda-
tion of her similar concept of poetic language: ". . . we can think of language as it is, as we
use it—as a process in which motion and relationship are always present."

From her earliest poems, she exhibited a tendency to reach out to her readers, to
touch them, somehow, in a more immediate, less cerebral way, perhaps, than that which
she traditionally identified with the reading of poetry. Before she could ever articulate
what she was doing, she sought to create that non-static, process-oriented sense of
motion and relationship within the dramatic scenarios that many of her poems utilized.
In "Effort at Speech Between Two People," for instance, from her first volume, *Theory of
Flight*, she rescued the narrative persona from the prison of the text by allowing it to
speak in a movingly direct way to the reader: "Take my hand. Speak to me," the narrator
implores in closing. It was a tactic guaranteed to ensure that the reader could not remain
unmoved by the reading of the poem; whether one was infuriated (and many were) by
such an invasive, personalizing tone of address, or whether one was emotionally devas-
tated by the sudden collapsing of the intellectual and mental worlds that generally served
to separate reader and poet, Rukeyser's discovery was that a reader could be made to
respond more directly, could be made aware of him- or herself as being in relationship
with the poet during the act of reading the poem.

"Both artist and audience create, and both do work on themselves in creating," was
how she phrased it in her prose work of 1949, *The Life of Poetry*. "A work of art is one
through which the consciousness of the artist is able to give its emotions to anyone who
is prepared to receive them."

It follows, then, that the writing of poetry was not—in fact, could not be, for her—

an individual or isolated creative act removed from other such acts. Although she wrote a number of ars poetica pieces during her long career, perhaps it is "To Enter that Rhythm Where the Self is Lost," from *Waterlily Fire* (1962) that best expresses her holistic approach to poetry writing, and the terribly complex, almost ineffable ideas that she held about the imaginative and emotional connections between poet and reader. To acknowledge the interrelatedness of all things, to render poetically one's own place in the dynamic systems of human life, was the writer's task. The reader's task, in reading the poem, was to enter into a system with the poet, to give it the gas, in a way to fire it up, and to get it going. *Where* poet and reader were going was toward a further exploration of that huge system—human experience—that subsumed both of them. Given that kind of content, it is no wonder at all that Rukeyser persistently refused to see poetry as an act removed in any way from other meaningful human acts. To write or to read a poem was to be born anew to the possibility of our interrelatedness, to experience, as the poem says, "That blind moment, midnight, when all sight/begins, and the dance itself is all our breath,/and we ourselves the moment of life and death." For Muriel Rukeyser, it was an all or nothing proposition. To write a poem was to be alive, to *know* that one was alive, to experience "the self as vision," and to understand that the vision of the self is the vision of others—that one lives among others, committing equally creative, equally useful acts; writing poems, making love, giving birth.

by Kate Daniels

For a Blow Up Doll Found in a Canal

Nothing could whiten
the brown opaque face
of the canal that flowed
beside me, not even
a slow dance of clouds
slumped together against the light.
It was there I saw
your V of flesh colored legs
floating inverted,
plastic toes pointed heavenward.
I pulled you out by your vinyl hair,
rinsed with silt and rain.
Mud fringed your face and mouth,
stunned into a perpetual O,
as if you looked out
from the peeling irises
of marble blue eyes,
saw what we were and what we did,
and you were constantly amazed.
Maybe it was a question
your flexible lips made
or maybe just terror
in that frozen red lipped O.

I gave you a name
because you had once held
the essence of blossoms and smog
that we all exhale,
because someone had kissed the soft pillows
of your air filled breasts,
because you had known rape and tenderness,
because I was like you once,
soft, pliant, and so adaptable.

I carried you home
and buried you under a flowering plum,
mud-caked orphan of my sex,
gave back your punctured, flattened body
to the cool earth
where you could rest,
deep among the looping roots,
your amazed plastic mouth refusing to lie,
refusing to decompose.

I WANT TO READ AND WRITE POETRY THAT BREATHES; BREATHES THROUGH THE MUSIC, BREATHES through the meaning. That means poetry taking place in and out of the world—poetry that has its feet, not just on the ground, but in the mud. Because poetry is dirt under your fingernails, and between your toes, and a recognition of the beauty and terror contained in the process itself, which is really the act of living.

This is poetry that is not alienated from our inner lives, not separate and compartmentalized, like a subject to be studied for a semester; but an integrated and fully realized part of ourselves.

By entering poetry, I have learned to trust myself more, and the rightness of failed memory; to let imagination play in the mine field of memory. Learning to believe in what we can't see, touch, taste, smell or hear involves trusting in memory and imagination, trusting in a force greater than our intellect or senses, and continuing to live in a state of amazement.

Dennis Saleh

The Unconscious

Expect the swollen gorge behind everything.
Expect taking in your hands
at least one of your parents
torn open to reveal what is inside.
Expect your conception, the wall you tear away from,
the dark burst ending nothing.
Plan loss. Plan having no room.
Plan slipping to your knees and fear
welling around your knees rising.
Now find the names for everything.
Now talk at last.
Say "Choking," say you are choking,
infancy is choking, childhood is choking,
your body is the throat your blood rushes to
flow from, your body stutters,
now it will never be over.
Realize the rest of your life will be like rain
falling far above you.
Realize Jesus warned you.
Realize you are being lied to,
that at any moment someone will bend to you
and whisper "I was here before you who am I."

POETRY OFTEN SEEMS TO COME FROM OUT OF NOWHERE. A POET WILL SPEAK OF NOT KNOWING
how, or why, he wrote a poem, of its surprising nature; that is, the wellspring of the poem
is unknown. In the modern parlance of the mind, another word for the unknown is the
"unconscious," and this poem is a kind of working catalogue of hidden recesses in the
mind: the proverbial experiences of infancy and childhood, the forgotten, the repressed.
If science may be thought of as a kind of poetry of measurements, then poetry might be
considered a kind of science of the unknown. Thus, a poem will seek to bring to precise
expression something previously unstated. In this respect, then, the last line of the poem
might be read, "This is here inside you. What is it about."

Sometimes Mysteriously

Sometimes in the evening when love
tunes its harp and the crickets
celebrate life, I am like a troubadour
in search of friends, loved ones,
anyone who will share with me
a bit of conversation. My loneliness
arrives ghostlike and pretentious,
it seeks my soul, it is ravenous
and hurting. I admire my father
who always has advice in these matters,
but a game of chess won't do, or
the frivolity of religion.
I want to find a solution, so I
write letters, poems, and sometimes
I touch solitude on the shoulder
and surrender to a great tranquility.
I understand I need courage
and sometimes, mysteriously,
I feel whole.

IN THE POEM, "SOMETIMES MYSTERIOUSLY," THE THEME OF LONELINESS APPEARS. I THINK IT IS a theme that pervades all of my poetry. However, here it takes a different turn. It finds a solution. Before it was madness or the edge of madness that seemed to rule over most everything I wrote. I could there tap into my unconscious freely. And thus, living in a fantastic world, I conjured many visions and idiosyncrasies into a poem. Nothing seemed to be studied seriously or in any depth. Feeling ran around freely.

I don't know if I write better poetry now, but I do write less and now the problem is not madness I have to deal with, but sanity. Now, I am more seriously looking for answers and being quiet; I am more concerned with an affirmation of life rather than just a negative irresponsibility. I am moving in the direction of a responsible self rather than a self betrayed, so to speak, by life.

Now, in a kind of self-revelation, I sum up my philosophy of all these years, what I have learned from the suffering and wandering lost in a negative world. In "Sometimes Mysteriously," I speak of a new found freedom, a kind of religion without religion—tranquility and solitude, and the idea of being at peace with oneself. This is no statement on how to live positively, but a sincere effort on my part to tie all loose ends up and venture forth with a clean slate, somewhat like a person facing a holocaust and surviving. No matter how negative life might seem to become there is always that ray of hope, whether it be a woman, friends, family or the mysterious forces that mold us into becoming a survivor. For what could be worse than losing one's mind and having so many years at rebuilding?

Thus, poetry assumes a larger role—one of being saved, discovery of self, the responsibility it brings having thus embraced humanity in all its good and all its dirt and corruption. Knowing and having lived in darkness, one can savor the light and better experience that life which is both darkness and light. So loneliness appears microscopic as one of man's problems. It can either get better or worse. Life's flame can either be extinguished or kept ablaze and the great responsibility that ensues. . . .

I live because I want to. Because I have nothing and because I have everything. And if we endure life, how better we can appreciate death. Poets die different deaths, to each his own fate. Poetry helps us endure. To say we've lived is the great accomplishment. Alas, having lived through it all.

Abandoned Railway Station

The agent's office like an abbey chancel.
The smell of wood smoke from the baggage stalls.
Large empty walls, and water-stain,
Ultramarine, like a fresco of Perseus,
Hand in hand, fleeing the golden falchion.

The silence of thousands of last goodbyes.
A dried ink pad. Stanchioned ceiling.
And a cognate, terra-cotta dust over
Everything, with an on-tiptoe atmosphere
Of a *boule de neige* before it's shaken.

An Art of Poetry: Postscript to "Abandoned Railway Station"

THE APPEAL OF AN ABANDONED PLACE—ESPECIALLY A PLACE THAT HAS FORMERLY SERVED AS A threshold between two other worlds—is its nagging, habitual dislocation, its *buried erotics* (the urgencies of what's-not-there), a fantasy that travels back in time and forward in psychological space. For while abandoned structures maintain the imprint of *their* earlier lives, they also serve to project us forward into a revery on those myriad moments of arrival and departure that eventually come to define *our* lives. That is part of the mysterious set of relations we've established between memory, reality, and dream (or, if you prefer, between the tradition, the poet, and the imagination): the past at the brink of becoming the present; the present at the brink of becoming the future. The "on-tiptoe atmosphere/Of a *boule de neige* before it's shaken."

Perhaps poetry, or at least lyric poetry, may be characterized by the two central illusions that define the nature of a *boule de neige*: the still moment disturbed into being (a wash of images across the reader's eye), and the following slow contraction of time as consciousness settles back into place (for what does the snowfall signify, except the poignant rhythms of a dreaming mind?).

Looking back, I suspect that it's a similar experience of time that first attracted me to poetry, and I doubt if over the years that original attraction has changed very much. What I loved then, what I love now, is that aura of heightened animation with which poetry tends to surround itself (the syllables of a line of verse like the snowfall of a *boule de neige*)—as if, not the atmosphere, but the subject itself were momentarily stirred to life. As if the mind might actually sustain that life. And since whatever we love informs the spirit of whatever we make, I can imagine (though I cannot explain) how my poems already know what they want even before I write them. Which is another way of saying that poetry's art remains for me a form of capitulation—to what I earlier called the buried erotics of what's-not-there—a form of submission to the poem itself. Poetry's art remains for me a form of saying what the poem thinks.

Dennis Schmitz

Because the Eye is a Flower Whose Root
is the Hand

the zoo raccoon lifts its food pellet,
& out of Genesis,

the Flemish tapestry Eve shows
the apple is an object

instinct truculently makes Art.
Look & look on your knees in the small

yard as you work
out the fallen earring (its coral

a tapestry knot)
from the knotted clover. Each green

clinging in the clover dozens
is a claim for Art, is a way for the earring

to survive as praise
for a way of looking.

Ignorance

THE ARS POETICA POEM IS BY DEFINITION AN IRONIC GESTURE. ITS NARCISSISM EMBODIES THE contraries of the writing experience. In the writing process, the poet talks to things and answers back in his/her own voice—a schizophrenia. Another paradox: a poet must surrender to the literal in order to imagine, to "see." I wanted this poem to hold out the food pellet and Art's apple, to find the earring in a progressive seeing. The manner of the search and the thing sought are the same thing. The earring, finally, either reverts to being an artifact of Nature or is claimed as an artifact by Nature, and one finds it only by giving in to Nature's way.

Re-enter the world on hands and knees—it is the writing process, whose first step is suspending judgement, holding out for "ignorance" that dignifies the poet because it means submitting to the materials, not putting aside one's personal failings, for instance, but working through them, naming things, naming oneself over again. The Japanese Zen poet Shinkichi Takahashi says, "I don't think the world reveals itself, it is we who reveal ourselves through proper relationship to it—when awakened."

The temptation of the Biblical Eve is solipsism. Art must resist it. How to accept the apple? The poem seems to suggest that Eve and the raccoon offer a kind of communion too.

The French poet Pierre Emmanuel affirms the paradoxical nature of writing. "My great force in my art," he says, "was first and foremost: ignorance. I fell in love only with what spoke to me." The rigor in writing poetry is to continue to maintain ignorance while at the same time applying the discipline of composition.

Lip's Lounge

They answer the phone there Lips
and lean on it. Where the tongue
goes to curl the L, I don't know,
but the i is long enough to ride
and the s rolling the p enacts
the word rippling the silence
it reverberates into. My stomach
decides, whatever doesn't have
lips wants them. Even a tongue
wants another tongue all its own.
Mine, alone in the mouth, wants
out. Lips says the bartender to
the phone and my tongue comes
out, hangs out of bed. I get
it back in, I use my hand, then
set my legs off across the room.
I like how they lip along,
how they lean in together on
the pool table and a bank shot
kissed just so the slow roll
slits the pocket clean. I'm
ready now to take the calls,
be the man who does the word.
I want the word. I practice,
curl my legs around the table
legs, inhale, lay the words in
air to air. Someday the word
will come without a sound.

I WOULD LIKE TO SAY THAT I SAT DOWN TO WRITE AN ARS POETICA POEM. FAR FROM IT. TO TRY
to fashion such a poem directly would intimidate me. I backdoored the tradition by try-
ing to express the delight I felt sitting at the bar at Lip's Lounge in Somerville, New Jersey
when the bartender, answering the phone, said, "Lips." How he exuberantly drew out the
sound riveted my attention.

Going with the delight drew me out on paper to a place where I had the opportu-
nity to say what I wanted to be: "be the man who does the word." And I wanted to
apprentice the art of poetry writing so well that "Someday the word would come with-
out a sound." The poem that is natural, effortless, at least in appearance. The craft be so
wedded to the thrust that the poem reads without a blink, without the slightest wince at
the poet intruding.

"Lip's" is spelled with an apostrophe in the title because the bar belonged to, and
may still belong to, Patsuela Lipscom. I went back to Lip's Lounge with the completed
poem and, with the gall of youth, presented it to the owner, who not only accepted it
without the slightest quizzical gesture but also put it up over the bar, saying that she
would frame it. I was so flattered that I had no idea how lucky I was.

Eve Shelnutt

Nature, One Might Say

A man with emerald birds for hair.
A man with emerald birds for hair
reading a book engraved in metal,
a large world hidden behind those words:
how dignified it is, how austere
in its workings. I want
to throw my head back, ask, Is this
a madhouse, all things just as you please?
We unpack the heroic virtues, say
"Sleep well" and, turning, recite
the words about parting: *safe, safe.* It's
definite: We shall not see one another
again. No, no a thousand times no
we never shall. Yet all my life
I have liked listening for something
that doesn't like to make a sound.
To possess the fabulous goods: the wheels,
the gleaming doorknobs, to watch them
shiver under my hands into silence. . . .
Notice: everything seems to be
asleep, even the horses graceful
and dense. I walk quickly
past the trees smothered in dusk.
If I made him a present of all adornments,
seriously, so he would never look into
a mirror, could he sleep garlanded
by my breathing?

IN ONE OF HER POEMS, ELIZABETH BISHOP WROTE, "I ADMIRE COMPRESSION, LIGHTNESS, AGILI-ty,/ all rare in this loose world," a line I recognized early as expressive of qualities I admire in Bishop's poetry that I also wanted in my own.

Now I think that I might want her to have added the word *deceptive* after *agile* for what would be an interesting juxtaposition to the words *rare* and *loose*, except of course agility suggests something of deception. The act of deception is motion, objects flashing on the way to being hidden, not absence itself. The magician's coin always resurfaces, simply in a different place.

*

Should an ars poetica poem look like one? Many lovely ones do, but I doubt I could ever write one. In fact, I doubt I would ever write a poem intentionally about esthetics, for I would immediately feel the weight of my intentions. For me the compression in poetry arises from my mind leaping, cat-burglar-like, from one idea to another. I like jaggedness in art, a sense of its being swept into a satchel on the run.

I'm after that point in this poem, the narrator asking "Is this a madhouse, all things just as you please?" since the seriousness of the book engraved in metal, holding its words hostage, is the antithesis to a world perceived as mad. Has the poet placed emerald birds—a sort of crown—on his head deliberately? I suspect so. In this poem, the fact denigrates the poet of beloved.

What I admire about Bishop's work is the way it suggests a poet whose "confession" was that she observed the world as its intimate. Poetry for her must have been simply an extension, almost a reflex, which the work that the poems obviously were preserves, as if not to capture in her poetry the lightness and agility that were her visual impulse would belittle nature and herself in it.

An ars poetica poem is, for me, part of "the fabulous goods" that I would like to watch shiver into silence, for I don't suppose that I do see the world as mad so much as misconstructed as mad. It might be useful to cease engraving anything in metal. I like silence because I distrust language and the posturing that attends so much of its use. All of Wallace Stevens' weight is counterbalanced by play, or play is its weight.

Strange, no doubt, to use Stevens as an example here, but I have always read most avidly not his "relaxations of the known" but "this old man selling oranges." When Stevens enters "boldly" the interior world, he brightens the exterior; it becomes brilliant. I have *seen* the jar in Tennessee a thousand times since reading his poem, and a thousand times before passed by it unseeing.

Ours is, anyway, a different world than Stevens', far less "agile." Even the horses "graceful and dense" seem to exist in shadow, appropriated to an interior before they have cantered.

I am tired of over-self-consciousness in our poetry; my *ear* is too accustomed to the contemporary poet's rhetorical gestures that remind us of at least *this* sensitive observer-recorder on duty, no matter how enervated and enervating the world seems to the read-er. "Please come flying" is so often Bishop's invitation, so infrequently ours. We seem as readers and writers to have our hands perpetually on our foreheads, our ennui rising like fever. Our ennui becomes our adornment, at which we stare in the mirror. Or like Manuelzinho, Bishop's half squatter, half tenant, we have "left out the decimal points" until our "columns stagger."

These days, when reading poetry, I have begun to ask myself if I would like to take a walk with a poet. Where would we be heading and how lightly would we go over what is left of nature?

Problems with the Story

The story was too long.

Before you told it, you forgot it.

Before the snake unwound
his infinite body
from around the tree,
the head forgot where he was going.

The story had too many beginnings.

If you stepped through a door
twelve others might open.

Did anyone have time?

The story, the story, whose was it?

Did someone else own it too?

The story knotted in the throat of a finch.

Sometimes the story felt cold after you told it.

The story might make his mother nervous.

This was only a translation of the story I heard
through a small crack while sleeping.

This was not the best story.

Angels and bells did not follow this story
but still, I had to tell it.

It was the only chance I had
to find you.

SOMETIMES EACH POEM SEEMS A VOTE FOR THE IMPOSSIBLE: NO, THIS ISN'T IT, QUITE, BUT THIS is close to it, or close to something, an act of approaching the ineffable by one more intimate path. Giant silent forests enclose each sentence. It would be easy not to speak at all. Stories being what they are, immense and unfathomable in their entirety—how easy to avoid. Easy, but doomed. For once you have entered that ring of voices which finds some use and light in any telling, nothing else will do. Each lost word a crumpled twig underfoot. Each poem a reaching. A slim branch with a sense of sky.

What amazes me most is how any *one* gives us so many *others*. This private startled glory of abundance. How, early on, we hope for height and breadth of a whole tree but later each flurry of leaves feels enough. The changing, intricate shadows. I felt "Problems with the Story" as a statement of faith although it seems to operate on the negative—a bouquet of possible excuses, held in the hand, gathered and acknowledged, till there are no more to check the impulse.

So many times and ways we might turn back, fall silent again. He said, she said. They might not. But there is that last line.

Prodigy

I grew up bent over
a chessboard.

I loved the word *endgame.*

All my cousins looked worried.

It was a small house
near a Roman graveyard.
Planes and tanks
shook its windowpanes.

A retired professor of astronomy
taught me how to play.

That must have been in 1944.

In the set we were using,
the paint had almost chipped off
the black pieces.

The white King was missing
and had to be substituted for.

I'm told but do not believe
that that summer I witnessed
men hung from telephone poles.

I remember my mother
blindfolding me a lot.

She had a way of tucking my head
suddenly under her overcoat.

In chess, too, the professor told me,
the masters play blindfolded,
the great ones on several boards
at the same time.

MANY YEARS AFTER THE EVENTS DESCRIBED IN THIS POEM, LATE ONE NIGHT IN 1972 IN Belgrade, an old relative produced the famous chess set in which the white King was still missing. I was very moved to see the man I hadn't seen in more than twenty years and equally moved to have the set back. We sat late into the night drinking wine while I played with the figures. Since I was sleeping elsewhere, I left at some point, taking the set along with me. I remember a long wait for the bus, and then a long ride to where I was staying. When I woke up the next day, I realized I had left the set on the bus. First I was mortified, and then kind of delighted. I'm sure whoever found it did not throw it away. I'd like to think some poor kid is sitting over it just as I was, making identical moves. In any case, its life continues now even more mysterious than it ever was.

Maurya Simon

Ars Poetica

Daredevil always, I took mine off first:
elbowed out of my shirt, shimmied from my skirt,
unshouldered my bra, dropped my panties—all
my garb tossed defiantly to the porch floor—
thus, stark in my naked geometry I stood,
shivering behind our trellised bougainvillea,
as Sunday cars sharked along Hermosa Avenue.
"Your turn," I began, but she'd already fled
behind the front door with her devising friend
who clutched my clothing to her chest.
I heard the latch snap loudly in its groove,
then their footsteps fanning out to other rooms,
as wildly they locked every entry to our house.
Sister, the sizzling curses I spit out that day
strung you up and quartered you until you bled
throughout eternity like a slaughtered pig.
Never had newborne words tasted so true and good:
Traitor! Sewer-slut! Scorpion shit! Shrew-lips!
I stood, one forearm smothering my breasts,
the other hand cupped over that darkened place
no eyes but mine had ever grazed before—
I called upon the gods of domestic revenge,
jazzy gods, bug-zappers, the gods of execution—
until laughter overcame me like thunder.
I wept, roared, choked on my nascent fury:
what a sight I offered to wide-eyed drivers
who circled the block once, twice, and again
to see that girlish apparition of mottled flesh
screaming out lungsful of invective.
When I grew hoarse, they let me back in.
Too late: my smoking voice lingered on the air,
my oaths lodged upon the vines—ruby-eyed,
razor-toothed, almost divine.

The Birth of Poetry

WELL, THIS IS INDEED A TRUE STORY. I MUST HAVE BEEN THIRTEEN OR SO—AN AWKWARD AGE,
even in the best (dressed) of circumstances. Being caught naked in public is not, of course,
a metaphor for feeling vulnerable: it's the epitome of vulnerability, the realization of a night-
mare. Being thirteen, nude, and stranded on a busy street exposed me, oddly enough, to a
hitherto unknown aspect of my own nature—namely, my need to verbalize my rage, to
sound my fury. If, as Emerson asserts, "all language is fossil poetry," then I was, at that chilly
moment, an archeologist who was re-inventing her own poetry. Some of the truest poems
arise from such *in extremis* moments; others give birth to various raw or sudden or crude
awakenings as they're being realized through language. Every poem, regardless of its merits,
re-enacts the birth of self. That's why poets are "makers," why we are harnessed to both the
sacred and the profane, why Emily Dickinson could crow so loudly in her poems, even as
she sat demurely, quietly in her room.

Gary Soto

Braly Street

Every summer
The asphalt softens
Giving under the edge
Of boot heels and the trucks
That caught radiators
Of butterflies.
Bottle caps and glass
Of the '40s and '50s
Hold their breath
Under the black earth
Of asphalt and are silent
Like the dead whose mouths
Have eaten dirt and bermuda.
Every summer I come
To this street
Where I discovered ants bit,
Matches flare,
And pinto beans unraveled
Into plants; discovered
Aspirin will not cure a dog
Whose fur twitches.

It's 16 years
Since our house
Was bulldozed and my father
Stunned into a coma . . .
Where it was,
An oasis of chickweed
And foxtails.
Where the almond tree stood
There are wine bottles
Whose history
Is a liver. The long caravan
Of my uncle's footprints
Has been paved
With dirt. Where my father
Cemented a pond
There is a cavern of red ants
Living on the seeds

The wind brings
And cats that come here
To die among
The browning sage.

It's 16 years
Since bottle collectors
Shoveled around
The foundation
And the almond tree
Opened its last fruit
To the summer.
The houses are gone,
The Molinas, Morenos,
The Japanese families
Are gone, the Okies gone
Who moved out at night
Under a canopy of
Moving stars.

In '57 I sat
On the porch, salting
Slugs that came out
After the rain,
While inside my uncle
Weakened with cancer
And the blurred vision
Of his hands
Darkening to earth.
In '58 I knelt
Before my father
Whose spine was pulled loose.
Before his face still
Growing a chin of hair,
Before the procession
Of stitches behind
His neck, I knelt
And did not understand.

Braly Street is now
Tin ventilators
On the warehouses, turning
Our sweat
Towards the yellowing sky;
Acetylene welders
Beading manifolds,
Stinging the half-globes
Of retinas. When I come
To where our house was,
I come to weeds
And a sewer line tied off
Like an umbilical cord;
To the chinaberry
Not pulled down
And to its rings
My father and uncle
Would equal, if alive.

FOR ME, STREETS HAVE ALWAYS MATTERED, AND WHEN I'M READY TO WRITE, READY TO SIT down, usually at our kitchen table, I conjure up inside my head an image of our old street, one that was torn down in the name of Urban Renewal at the beginning of the 1960s. It was, as some might imagine, a blighted area: a junkyard to the left of us, a pickle factory across the street, broom factory and warehouse of books and magazines down the alley, the almighty Sun-Maid Raisin refinery in the distance, and weed-choked vacant lots. These are pictures that I take into my work, both in poetry and prose, pictures that arouse a passion for the past, which I constantly haunt with an inventory list. They muster up a power inside me, a delicious feeling of memory, imagination and the willingness to care for the smallest of objects. It's not unusual for me to close my eyes for a moment or two, to see people and things in their place, from my father, dead now, and an uncle, also dead, to our dusty-white house, the bean-plants, the almond tree where I hung ridiculously by an army belt, the fishless pond, my uncle back from Korea sleeping in the sun porch. Nothing much happened. No one pushed ahead, no one got rich. Everyone leaned their sadness on fences, sat in twos and threes on porches, or, if you were younger, bobbed on car fenders, the music of Harry Belafonte in leather-wrapped radios. We all faced the street, that river of black asphalt, and kept our eyes busy on every car that passed. I spent my first six years running like a chicken from one dirt yard to another, and I can't think of a more curious or unadorned childhood. It's these images that I take to the page, whether the subject is that street or another street and time. It's these first images, these first losses when our street was leveled to the height of yellow weeds, that perhaps made me a writer. We lose our family, our loves, our places, and finally ourselves in our haunted end. I work to restore these losses, first with private, closed-eyed moments in which I see our lives as they were, simple and full, and later in the shape of poems and prose, when the subjects come alive on a street we all miss.

Diving for Atlantis
for Ada

In a flush of leafless gum and alder,
the old Fourth Street Y
where the run-off from swamps
and secret southern tides collects.
On cold afternoons,
the black kids come here to dive
for what one says is *Atlanta,*
an island floating miles beneath
the fractured basin of this pool,
loaded with all the precious stones
their mothers promised them
in lullabies. Like the gulls
or kingfishers cracking the slate swells
200 miles from here, down they go
shooting up again and again
through the wreath of bubbles
to the surface, screaming
found it, found it

Who in this city
smelling of scorched tobacco
and hickory dust would believe
what they can't see or sell,
so much water slipping through fingers?
Like the old woman lounging
on a faded towel, winter settles
into an armchair padded with dead leaves
and counts its treasure—
all the white faces glistening like dimes,
all the blacks bearing out
the same cold. But here,
a child in a pair of scissored trousers
leaps into the water and learns
to hold his breath until
the vision comes and the sunlight
slices him into every color.

Lady, the woman tells me, *Methodists*
don't take to water,
but I'm learning.
It's the Baptists who walk into lakes
and leave the rest of us
standing on the shore.

And I believe that even hers,
the heaviest earthbound body,
can hold air and float
on those seven veils of blue.
When I plunge headfirst,
joining her and all the others,
my flesh steeps and the steam rises
off the surface. I believe
that those who swim in winter
shed ghosts like these
whose sweet alum tears fall
to something larger, a sea
that never freezes over,
whose gentle pulse carries them
away from the Y, from this city,
to the shores of Atlanta
where, when they surface,
they will send for us.

I WANT MY POEMS TO SPRING FROM THE HEART AND TO CELEBRATE THE POWER OF THE IMAGI-
nation. This poem comes as close to doing this as anything I've written. It also takes this
task as its subject.

At the time I wrote "Diving for Atlantis," I was pregnant with my first child and living
in the South (North Carolina). The world around me seemed unbelievably vibrant and
intriguing. The children who swam around me at the local "Y" demonstrated what I had
already learned as a poet—that the imagination has an infinite capacity for transforming
one's identity and surroundings. Likewise, as the Methodist woman explains in the second
stanza, the qualities that make a person or place unique are also often worth our praise.

Just as the children dive into the water to look for the mythical city of Atlanta, the
poet must penetrate the layers of the imagination until the vision is realized.

Elizabeth Spires

The Woman on the Dump

Where was it one first heard of the truth? The the.
—Wallace Stevens

She sits on a smoldering couch
reading labels from old tin cans,
the ground ground down
to dirt, hard as poured cement.
A crowd of fat white gulls
take mincing, oblique steps
around the couch, searching for
an orange rind, a crab claw.
Clouds scud backward overhead,
drop quickly over the horizon,
as if weighted with lead sinkers.
The inside's outside here,
her "sitting room" *en plein air*:
a homey triad of chaise lounge,
tilting table, and old floor lamp
from a torn-down whorehouse,
the shade a painted scene
of nymphs in a naked landscape.
The lamp is a beautiful thing,
even if she can't plug it in,
the bare-cheeked, breathless
nymphs part of the eternal
feminine as they rush away
from streaming trees and clouds
that can't be trusted not to change
from man to myth and back again.

The dump's too real. Or not
real enough. It is hot here.
Or cold. When the sun goes down,
she wraps herself in old newspaper,
the newsprint rubbing off,
so that she *is* the news as she
looks for clues and scraps
of things in the refuse. The *the*
is here somewhere, buried
under bulldozed piles of trash.

She picks up a pair of old cymbals
to announce the moon, the pure
symbol, just coming up over there.
Abandoned bathtubs, sinks, and stoves
glow white—abstract forms
in the moonlight—a high tide
of garbage spawns and grows,
throwing long lovely shadows
across umplumbled ravines and gullies.
She'll work through the night,
the woman on the dump,
sifting and sorting and putting
things right, saving everything
that can be saved, rejecting
nothing, piles of tires
in the background unexhaustedly
burning, burning, burning.

"THE WOMAN ON THE DUMP" BEGAN AS A RESPONSE TO STEVENS' ARS POETICA "THE MAN ON the Dump" and takes as its epigraph the last line of Stevens' poem. As I worked on it, however, other ars poeticas came to mind and literary allusions crept in: to the classical tradition and Keats' Grecian urn (transformed into a painted lampshade of nymphs in a pastoral landscape) and to William Carlos Williams' remark in "Asphodel, That Greeny Flower" that "It is difficult/ to get the news from poems. . . ." Like Elizabeth Bishop's character Edwin Boomer in her allegory "The Sea & Its Shore," who "lived the most literary life possible," the woman on the dump lives in a world of letters (literal letters, such as one might find on tin cans and scraps of newsprint). She sees her task as a kind of creative ordering of chaos—it's almost housework but not quite. I hope the poem reconciles the spheres of domesticity and creativity so often opposed in the actual world but perhaps able to be fused in the world of imagination.

William Stafford

The Old Writers' Welcome to the New

Somewhere out there new light
is crossing a field. Our time, long
preparing for this, carefully comes near.
Without our knowing, our lives
have bent steadily toward this field,
and now we approach and bow down.

All that we welcomed and then forsook,
or lost by weakness, or by cruel time—
friends grown cold, family turned away,
Katherine whose face reflects even yet
when a train goes by, and old Lief
looking at us toward the end from his kennel—
these were needed so that this future could arrive.

Glad for this field, welcoming new light,
we embrace the loss and regret we must pay
all through our years, that Now may arrive,
that our story come true and be what it is,
again and again.

But oh our loves, happy goodbyes.

Ave ataque Vale: The Welcome and Farewell of Life

EVERYTHING I WRITE HAS IN IT, OR HOVERING BEHIND IT, OR READY TO CLAIM KINSHIP, AN adaptable prose explanation. I could go on forever and wind about my work its long source, being, and tending-forwardness. "The Old Poets Welcome to the New" has readily available in my mind such adjunct wordings. . . .

Early on, my tentative title was "Future Nostalgia." I was blundering my way among thoughts of how our various pasts—even the "bad" parts—were necessary for what we are approaching; our Now, with whatever of good or promise it has, grows from those pieces of life we have experienced. We let go in order to take hold.

And so I recognize—in terms of "new light" and a field—what is imminent, maybe a dawn, maybe an impending scene. My first group of lines makes sense to me with this overlay.

My second group of lines expands on the idea and puts it into a sequence of particulars (friends now gone, family, a person named Katherine, an old dog). I thrive on such a sequence; my poems live by touching these particular (but *emblematic*) parts of my (implied at least) own life.

And my last group of lines embraces those losses as necessary for the present that we welcome, identifying the Now of experience in terms of that new light, that field, mentioned in the beginning. And this relinquishing and taking up sequence has made something that happens again and again. (I feel a little diminished by my flat statement now while I am analyzing my poem—is that all that I am doing, I ask myself, belatedly, here in the "new light" of prose. . . .)

And in one last line I indulge myself with a yearning backward gesture. I can't without a fervent reach for them give up friends, family, Katherine, old Lief. And because it is a poem, because I reach with all my life, I have it all, the old loves, the present because it is here and yielding me *happy* goodbyes.

Gerald Stern

Another Insane Devotion

This was gruesome—fighting over a ham sandwich
with one of the tiny cats of Rome, he leaped
on my arm and half hung on to the food and half
hung on to my shirt and coat. I tore it apart
and let him have his portion, I think I lifted him
down, sandwich and all, on the sidewalk and sat
with my own sandwich beside him, maybe I petted
his bony head and felt him shiver. I have
told this story over and over; some things
root in the mind; his boldness, of course, was frightening
and unexpected—his stubbornness—though hunger
drove him mad. It was the breaking of boundaries,
the sudden invasion, but not only that, it was
the sharing of food and the sharing of space; he didn't
run into an alley or into a cellar,
he sat beside me, eating, and I didn't run
into a trattoria, say, shaking,
with food on my lips and blood on my cheek, sobbing;
but not only that, I had gone there to eat
and wait for someone. I had maybe an hour
before she would come and I was full of hope
and excitement. I have resisted for years
interpreting this, but now I think I was given
a clue, or I was giving myself a clue,
across the street from the glass sandwich shop.
That was my last night with her, the next day
I would leave on the train for Paris and she would
meet her husband. Thirty-five years ago
I ate my sandwich and moaned in her arms, we were
dying together; we never met again
although she was pregnant when I left her—I have
a daughter or son somewhere, darling grandchildren
in Norwich, Connecticut, or Canton, Ohio.
Every five years I think about her again
and plan on looking her up. The last time
I was sitting in New Brunswick, New Jersey,
and heard that her husband was teaching at Princeton,
if she was still married, or still alive, and tried
calling. I went that far. We lived
in Florence and Rome. We rowed in the bay of Naples
and floated, naked, on the boards. I started
to think of her again today. I still
am puzzled by the connection. This is another
insane devotion, there must be hundreds, although
it isn't just that, there is no pain, and the thought
is fleeting and sweet. I think it's my own dumb boyhood,

147

walking around with Slavic cheeks and burning
stupid eyes. I think I gave the cat
half of my sandwich to buy my life, I think
I broke it in half as a decent sacrifice.
It was this I bought, the red coleus,
the split rocking chair, the silk lampshade.
Happiness. I watched him with pleasure.
I bought memory. I could have lost it.
How crazy it sounds. His face twisted with cunning.
The wind blowing through his hair. His jaws working.

WHEN I THINK ABOUT "ANOTHER INSANE DEVOTION," WHEN I TALK ABOUT IT, I TEND TO
emphasize the relationship with the woman I loved and lived with, not the connection
with the cat that was the agency of so much terror and desperation and ambiguity. I am
always surprised, when I look at the poem itself, how critical the presence of the cat is. In
a sense, the poem is more about the cat than it is about the woman. He appears first (if
she's a he) and dominates the beginning as well as the end of the poem. In fact, from a
quantitative point of view, the cat "occupies" the first twenty lines and the last sixteen;
this in a poem that is fifty-eight lines long, which means there are about twenty-two lines
devoted to the woman. In the most obvious sense of the word, the cat represents the ars
poetica. He is irrational, independent, impulsive, amoral, and my equal—and antago-
nist—(and partner) in spite of his size. He is bold, stubborn, and rather human-like, as
he sits beside me eating his half of the sandwich. He is a little frightening, a little horri-
fying. At the end, cunning, godlike, almost indifferent. By comparison, the woman—she
was really a girl—is, as I look at the poem now—absolutely normal and conventional in
her behavior. Indeed, she exists, in the poem, as an extension of *my* feeling; she doesn't
generate—how shall I put it?—an independent and separate *mind* (forgive me), as the
cat does. We were in love, we were devoted to each other, we traveled through romantic
Italy, we made love in a rowboat, we "moaned in each other's arms." The only thing that
was unusual was that she was pregnant, with my child, when I left her, and I never saw
her again, though it would have been relatively easy to make contact, since her husband
was famous. That is the part where the cat enters; it touches of "cat."

I don't know what the poem is about. Maybe guilt, maybe memory, maybe happiness.
Some mythical process. Sacrifice, certainly. The life of art. It is one of ten or twenty poems
I have written where I'm governed—engulfed—by a greater presence. I have no embar-
rassment in saying it. I was in the hands of something else. The poem may be about the
creative process, as a good ars poetica should be, but it's a process that's larger than that
connected with the writing of a poem only. If I were a Jungian I would have a field day. God
knows the levels of meaning in the cat, if *I'm* the cat, who represented what, where my psy-
che was. I think what I admire in the poem is its honesty and its ruthlessness, its *disinter-
estness*, as Hazlitt would say, well, combined with its affection. I beg forgiveness of the girl—
her name was Kate—for not staying with her. It was the fifties, and that's the way things
were done. She had a husband; and I was engaged. I had a happy life; I have dear children.
We'll meet another day.

Gin

There's a mystery
By the river, in one of the cabins
Shuttered with planks, its lock
Twisted; a bunch of magazines flipped open,
A body. A blanket stuffed with leaves
Or lengths of rope, an empty gin bottle.
Put down your newspaper. Look out
Beyond the bluffs, a coal barge is passing,
Its deck nearly
Level with the water, where it comes back riding
High. You start talking about nothing,
Or that famous party, where you went dressed
As a river. They listen,
The man beside you touching his odd face
In the counter top, the woman stirring tonic
In your glass. Down the bar the talk's divorce,
The docks, the nets
Filling with branches and sour fish. Listen,
I knew a woman who'd poke a hole in an egg, suck
It clean and fill the shell with gin,
Then walk around disgusting people
Until she was so drunk
The globe of gin broke in her hand. She'd stay
Alone at night on the boat, come back
Looking for another egg. That appeals to you, rocking
For hours carving at a hollow stone. Or finding
A trail by accident, walking the bluff's
Face. You know, your friends complain. They say
You give up only the vaguest news, and give a bakery
As your phone. Even your stories
Have no point, just lots of detail: The room
Was long and bright, small and close, angering Gaston;
They turned away to embrace him; She wore
The color out of season,

She wore hardly anything at all; Nobody died; Saturday.
These disguises of omission. Like forgetting
To say obtuse when you talk about the sun, leaving
Off the buttons as you're sewing up the coat. So,
People take the little
They know to make a marvelous stew;
Sometimes, it even resembles you. It's not so much
You cover your tracks, as that they bloom
In such false directions. This way friends who awaken
At night, beside you, awaken alone.

WHEN I'M ASKED WHICH OF MY POEMS I MIGHT CONSIDER TO BE AN ARS POETICA, THERE ARE
two that leap to mind: the poem "Gin" from my first collection, *Hush*; and the poem "The
Man in the Yellow Gloves" from the book *No Heaven*.

"Gin" was written to be not only an *ars poetica* but an *ars vita* as well. At the time, I
was being accused of obscurity in my poetry—and in my personal life as well—and it
seemed time to address both issues. The poem is cast as a kind of mock murder mystery,
triggered by a story the poem's protagonist reads in a newspaper while sitting in a bar. A
few of life's odd mysteries get interwoven into the poem, and like much of life more ques-
tions are asked in the poem than are answered. The poem is, of course, full of "disguises
of omission." It's what I like to do in my work, to create some space in which mystery
might still exist. At least, this is the pleasure I look for constantly in other poets' poems,
and what I love best in poetry whenever I find it.

Word Silence

There's a flame like the flame of fucking
that longs to be put out: words are filings
drawn toward a vast magnetic silence.
The loins ask their usual question
concerning loneliness.
The answer is always a mountaintop
erasing itself in a cloud.
It's as if the mind keeps flipping
a coin with a lullaby on one side
and a frightening thrill on the other,
and if it lands it's
back in the air at once.
A word can rub itself rosy
against its cage of context,
starting a small fire in the sentence
and trapping for a moment
the twin scents of now and goodbye.
The sexual mimicry always surprises me:
the long dive the talky mind makes
into the pleasures of its native dark.
Like pain, such joy is locked
in forgetfulness, and the prisoner
must shout for freedom again and again.
Is that what breaks the sentences apart
and spreads their embers in a cooling silence?
The pen lies in the bleach of sunlight
fallen on the desk, ghost-sheet of a bed
turned back. If I look for a long time
into its wordlessness, I can see
the vestiges of something that I knew
dissolving. Something that I no longer know.
And there I sleep like an innocent
among the words I loved
but crushed for their inflammable perfumes.

To me, one of the durable mysteries of writing is the inconstancy of access I have to my own work. A poem often begins as an internal pressure, a dumb yearning for contact, for language: something wants to name itself. During the writing, I'm slave to the poem, bent on bringing it (whatever it is), clear and whole, into language that will hold a window in its mystery open forever. But how is it possible to live in a poem, be possessed by it, and then afterward not be able to remember how it was written? When a poem is finished, the surface closes over. How strange it is to read it then, as it withdraws into its new independence. The process seems to me almost sexual in its mechanism: a yearning, with or without specific object, becomes desire, becomes purpose, and that purpose is, ultimately, to exhaust itself, to pleasure itself in articulation but also to get to the end, which is a withdrawal back into silence, where there's nothing more to be said. And out of that silence comes a new, more refined, loneliness, which creates a new internal pressure. Or at least it's a *narrower* loneliness, one that is less ignorant of itself. That's what I learned by writing the poem.

Jon Veinberg

Stickball Till Dawn

It's always two hours to go on the night shift
When they return to me with their hollowed out knees
And low quick strides tilting the bricks of first base

Not knowing a bat from a broomstick, a sandal
From a spike, or the marquee that imagines their names
From the long sleeve of neon blinking red & gold & blue,

Eking out the only light left wedged
Between the gutted five and dime and Dr Pepper™ sign:
There's Fishface Walker cupping a butt

In the deep shaft of center field, his face
At each glowing puff, a shining clarity of salve
And crisscrossed scabs from taking too many headfirsts

Into the curb. There's Angel Ramirez
Outracing a ball that barely busts air, backpedaling
So fast sparks stream off his calloused heels

That when he hit the stolen Studebaker abandoned
In Tiger Alley we ran for the night watchman,
Caught between nods of solitaire and recurring blonds,

To pull out the silver hawked hood ornament galvanized
To his neck. He laid in a coma for three days
Before we brought him back, carried him up to the rooftop

Where in the dark chamber between the stars,
Confetti dripped from his pocket, a cat homing his lap,
He sipped from a straw and grunted his disapproval

In a language none of us could decipher
As if the heavens were echoing his groan at each shy blooper
That ricocheted off our embarrassed hands. Two hours to go

Before the sun breaks open the smoked rectangle
Of windows, carrying its pail of cracked light
To the scrub woman struggling with her keys

And after twenty-five years of waiting for light
And groping for grounders in the dark, I know the one-eyed skinny kid
Is still hugging the chalked map of second base, halfway there

Between the limbo of winning and losing, still timing his stride
For the last hard liner to right that'll stretch his fatherless legs
Toward that vague and dizzy notion of home, while the sun

Climbs the broken back of Angel Ramirez, sending wisps
Of brown mill air, the foam of furnaces, and the grilled ashes
Of summer spinning off toward a paused and different sky.

On the back of my book I am rewarded with a blurb that uses the words "drama" and "imagination," two words that always held negative connotations while growing up. For instance, in the fifth grade, I was absorbed in devising a plan for dropping cherry bombs into our public school restroom. A perfect strategy when completed which I could share with my classmates in the simultaneous sensation of seeing and hearing shit and porcelain explode. This act was always met with failure, admonition, and the principal's recurring lecture on the parameters of drama and imagination. There are other examples: the harpooning of goldfish with a number two lead pencil after reading *The Old Man and the Sea*, the transplanting of rattlesnake tails onto the body of a turtle in hopes of generating a better way to crawl. One could say that I now write poems because I am being rewarded for things I was once punished for. One could say but it wouldn't be true.

In "Stickball Till Dawn" a group of boys are playing a typical game in a forbidden place and time, a place and time of their own devising. Whether they know it or not they are sensing human drama unfold. It is not unlike the act of writing poems that these boys should return as poets to rehash this experience over a few beers, to return to a point of reference where their passion for a silly game has surpassed their fear of darkness. The journey they take is through the myriad sounds and symbols of each one's specific memory. The trouble is that the journey never ends in the same collective place, or they, as a group, would fly there to quench their imaginative thirsts without ever having to set foot on the ground. They have been lucky enough to begin at a similar place, a spot of familiar experience. The bombing of toilets in a grammar school bathroom or the playing of stickball under the meager arc of neon isn't a bad place to start dramatizing and embellishing.

Ann Vnucak

Ars Poetica

Starlings conduct themselves
through air that is not moved
by the purpled lashings
of wings or the whipping
of the bodies against
the day's sack of ashen light.
Heaven holds so little
that migratory flocks
are known to collide
and bring down the pumping
muscle of a jet . . .

       Downed from that view
of the stars toward which
Ovid tilted the tip
of the human heart
while my own heart insists
upon crawling into
caves ored with memory.
I squint like a child
with longitude of eye
still too short to refract
the tricks of space and light.

So I renovate the
dim temple of the past
into a sauna, each
life dropped behind by time
is reconstituted
as a glowing stone
veined with story.

Yet I can't remember
the rhythm-and-catch of
my first lover's breath,
nor recall the first
color of my mother's
hair now dusked to the hue
of pressure-treated wood.
At birth, my eyelids, like
torn wings, and my nose
and chin, mis-assembled
in a beak-like clench,

shielded me from her eyes
until I was revised
with steel quills and
blots of lapis bruises.

If, as Borges believed,
every word, in the end,
traces the outlines
of the face, then all
stories might be the same
one . . . To keep paring
away the stoney flesh
with the lift-and-drag
of feathery breath
before we dropwheel down
from the milky hold
of heaven's lapless stars.

THE COMPOSITION OF MY "ARS POETICA" INVOLVES THE ARTICULATION OF THE SOLUTION TO THE tension of the initial impulse, in this case a comment by Jorge Luis Borges. Unstrict syllabics are used only with the express purpose of facilitating a condensed, to-the-point poem rhythmically aided by a short line. Borges' thought along with some lines from Ovid's *Metamorphoses* set up a chain of association among elements I had already gathered in a notebook or had just mentally tabbed. A *Smithsonian* article on bird feather identification yielded that, in 1960, a jet out of Boston actually collided with flocks of migrating starlings and the ensuing crash killed 62 people. This event helped change FAA flight patterns and redesigned aircraft. I am immensely interested in the physical world and in the human capacity for coping with (in) that real world. This coping capacity is the core and spirituality of our existence, our link and tether to God. Transcendence itself is a coping mechanism as is continuity, i.e., our pasts.

Formal structure is a tool and not a given for me and so is subservient to subject matter and the evolving effect. Language is rooted in emotional impact; it "appears" in the work, usually, rather than allowing itself to be "dug up." Once on paper, language may not want to leave. It becomes that lonely bachelor uncle with all the stories he's seen, or that exasperating in-law living out her last five lines in this particular poem. Poetry shows how to cope through its transcendent language which, like most of life, refuses to be controlled. Poetry shares its grace to transcend through that subject matter that language (particularly metaphor) and strategies of argument and structure render interesting, intelligent and powerful.

Song and Story
for Allen Grossman

The girl strapped in the bare mechanical crib
does not open her eyes, does not cry out.
The glottal tube is taped into her face;
bereft of sound, she seems so far away.
But a box on the stucco wall, wired to her chest,
televises the flutter of her heart—
news from the pit—her pulse rapid and shallow,
a rising line, except when her mother sings,
outside the bars: whenever her mother sings
the line steadies into a row of waves,
song of the sea, song of the scythe

      old woman by the well, picking up stones
      old woman by the well, picking up stones

When Orpheus, beating rhythm with a spear
against the deck of the armed ship, sang
to steady the oars, he borrowed an old measure:
broadax striking oak, oak singing back,
the churn, the pump, the shuttle sweeping the warp
like the waves against the shore they were pulling toward.
The men at the oars saw only the next man's back.
They were living a story—the story of desire,
the rising line of ships at war or trade.
If the sky's dark fabric was pierced by stars,
they didn't see them; if dolphins leapt from the water,
they didn't see them. Sweat beaded their backs
like heavy dew. But whether they came to triumph
or defeat, music ferried them out
and brought them back, taking the dead and wounded
back to the wave-licked, smooth initial shore,
song of the locust, song of the broom

      old woman in the field, binding wheat
      old woman by the fire, grinding corn

When Orpheus, braiding rushes by the stream,
devised a song for the overlords of hell
to break the hearts they didn't know they had,
he drew one from the olive grove—
the raven's hinged wings from tree to tree,
whole flocks of geese crossing the ruffled sky,
the sun's repeated arc, moon in its wake:
this wasn't the music of pain. Pain has no music,
pain is a story: it starts,
Eurydice was taken from the fields.
She did not sing—you cannot sing in hell—
but in that viscous dark she heard the song
flung like a rope into the crater of hell,
song of the sickle, song of the hive

    old woman by the cradle, stringing beads
    old woman by the cradle, stringing beads

The one who can sing sings to the one who can't,
who waits in the pit, like Procne among the slaves,
as the gods decide how all such stories end,
the story woven into the marriage gown,
or scratched with a stick in the dust around the well,
or written in blood in the box on the stucco wall—
look at the wall:
the song, rising and falling, sings in the heartbeat,
sings in the seasons, sings in the daily round—
even at night, deep in the murmuring wood—
listen—one bird, full-throated, calls to another,
little sister, frantic little sparrow under the eaves.

LIKE OTHER POETS, I HAVE WRITTEN NOT ONE BUT MANY ARS POETICA POEMS OVER THE YEARS—particular stones in the river. Their differences are instructive and make me chary of unambiguous prose. Recently my preferred definition of poetry has been *truth set to music,* and at age fifty, I'm back where I began, trusting more, loving more, the music. But perhaps I only need to think I think so, in order to follow the current around the bend?

Diane Wakoski

With Words
for Tony

Poems come from incomplete knowledge.
From the sense of seeing
an unfinished steel bridge
that you'd like to walk across,
your imaginary footprints floating like pieces
of paper,
where the metal ends,
on the cold water
far below;
or the moon disappearing
behind a cloud
just when you could almost
see the face
of the man standing next
to you
in the olive trees;

And consequently,
I write about those
whose hands
I've touched once,
trying to remember
which fingers had the rings
on them,
speculating from a few words
what the dialogue of a lifetime
would have been,
making the facts up
out of the clouds of breath we release
on a winter night.
How can I
then
make a poem for you?
whose skillful hand
could make expert
blueprints
of all my bones?
There is no need
for a bridge between us;

we sleep on the same side of the bed.
Your mustache,
inherited from some stealthy Cossack
who kissed your great-great-great-
grandmother
and slid his icy cock between her warm
legs one night
is no mystery
to me.
I can relive
its history,
drawing lines all over my body.
I have no questions
either
about your powerful legs,
arms,
back,
or the quick mind
which leads the body around on a leash.

Forgive me then,
if the poems I write
are about the fragments,
the broken bridges,
and unlit fences
in my life.
For the poet,
the poem
is not
the measure
of his love. It is
the measure
of all he's lost, or
never seen,
or what has no life,
unless he gives it life
with words.

Ars Poetica

IT'S CLEAR TO ME, IN THIS LAST DECADE OF THE TWENTIETH CENTURY, THAT POETRY IS MORE like religion than like art or philosophy. It has a variety of histories, none of which offers a consistent argument for poetry as intellectual discourse, ideology, entertainment, something recognizably beautiful or wise, or something needed or even desired by the world. Like religion, a need for poetry has to be perceived; a belief is required to maintain its practice, and unlike visual art or music it does not offer aesthetic satisfaction unless one believes in and/or is knowledgeable about its particular structures or functions.

Since I am one of the believers in poetry, many of my poems are rather like missionary tracts, trying to describe what poetry is or could mean to others who don't believe in it. While I don't believe that poetry at its best is about poetry, I do believe that all poetry leads us to perfect or beautiful forms (in a Platonic sense), and that some times to talk about the art of poetry in a poem is a way to lead the reader to understanding beauty or wisdom, truth, or some other ideal. Poetry, like religion, is a way of revealing these perfect forms, God if you will; yet in my poems, when I use the word "poem," I want the reader to understand I mean the greater word "life" or the smaller word "voice," both of which imply that trying to understand what makes poetry is really the attempt to understand what makes a good life, what place voice, or song, or the word, speech, have in structuring and completing one's life.

In my poem "With Words," which is a love poem more than a tract on writing poetry, I'd like to persuade the reader that poetry's very value is that it is not applicable to daily satisfactory life, that it is something greater, helping us to cope with the missing rather than with what is already there. I believe this is a version of beauty that is not always obvious, thus needs some preaching. I also want to imply that no matter how physically good and satisfactory one's life is there is still something missing, because life cannot be perfect or whole, even for a millionaire, a movie star, royalty, or genius. To talk like this is to preach, whereas what I attempt to do in my poem is not to preach but to offer an emotional argument for this set of ideas, couched in the satisfaction of a relationship that balances with other less satisfactory realizations of endings or loss or simple inadequacy.

Why is this poetry rather than philosophy or religion? For me, it is poetry because it is something to say, to sing, to chant, as much as the offering of an idea or ideology. The trope of the lover whose love makes it impossible for her to practice her best skill can be seen as an argument, but it is much more effective as an image, an emotional offering. Or so I believe.

Even though this poem is overtly about the art of poetry, its inner voice is emotional, crying out against the overly-practical world, begging for the acceptance of something ideal, in this case poetry, which in fact is useless, not practical or valuable in achieving worldly ends. I suppose I see "With Words" as akin to Whitman's "To The Learned Astronomer." The poem's doctrine is not anti-materialistic, though it is anti-pragmatic, thus it presents an emotional appeal rather than a rational one. Surely we need a current admonition against giving up something like poetry, which has become an almost invisible art in our culture, precisely because poetry does not seem to have any pragmatic use and it doesn't conform to current ideas of beauty, entertainment, or Quantum age wisdom.

161

The Impossible

Winter's last rain and a light I don't recognize
through the trees and I come back in my mind
to the man who made me suck his cock
when I was seven, in sunlight, between boxcars.
I thought I could leave him standing there
in the years, half smile on his lips,
small hands curled into small fists,
but after he finished, he held my hand in his
as if astonished, until the houses were visible
just beyond the railyard. He held my hand
but before that he slapped me hard on the face
when I would not open my mouth for him.

I do not want to say his whole hips
slammed into me, but they did, and a black wave
washed over my brain, changing me
so I could not move among my people in the old way.
On my way home I stopped in the churchyard
to try and find a way to stay alive.
In the branches a redwing flitted, warning me.
In the rectory, Father prepared
the body and blood for mass
but God could not save me from a mouthful of cum.
That afternoon some lives turned away from the light.
He taught me how to move my tongue around.
In his hands he held my head like a lover.
Say it clearly and you make it beautiful, no matter what.

Why I Write Like I Write: Notes towards an Ars Poetica

Fanatics have their dreams. . . .
— John Keats

THE PARADOX OF MY PARTICULAR PATHOLOGY AS A WRITER IS THAT THE WAR RUINED MY LIFE and in return gave me my art. The war robbed me of my boyhood and forced me, at eighteen years old, to bear too much witness to the world, to what men were capable of doing to other men and to children and to women.

The war took away my life and gave me poetry in return. The war taught me irony. That I among the others would survive is ironic. All of my heroes are dead. That's the particular paradox of my experience as a writer. The fate the world has given to me is to write so beautifully as to draw the others into the horror.

I was up North on Highway One past Hue. I must have had some bad water because I got sick. I shit and vomited. In my stomach a black snake grew. They sent me to the rear, to An Khe, and I slept in twisted sheets on a cot until some man threw a book at me and said Read this boy. I was eighteen. This was called The Republic of Vietnam. Republic, God save us.

I had never read a book straight through in my life. I could not say the names in this book even out loud to myself, but I kept reading, the dream of the suffering horse pulling me into the story. I read Raskolnikov's letter over and over. Something snapped into place in my brain.

"I fear in my heart that you may have been visited by the latest unfashionable unbelief," Pulcheria wrote to her son.

She was writing to me as well. I don't know why the words made sense, 1968, the war raging all around us, the air filled with screams. The world conspired to put me there, in that war, in that province of blood, at that moment, so the man could drop the book on my bunk without looking at me. The book that was my link to another world, that was my bridge into a space blown wide open with a light that filled my brain.

I came from a house of no books. I ran away from the steel mill town and its grit to the war. I was not headed in the direction of books, but there was a moment reading and rereading *Crime and Punishment* that morning, my stomach raw from bad water, my nerves blown out, my life on a kind of wire or string, that I must have glimpsed the enormous possibilities of expression because I was jarred out of one way of thinking into another and from that moment the enormity and the impossibility of the struggle at hand revealed itself in a kind of splendor or order that vanished as quickly as it appeared. I have looked for it ever since. It has become my way to find it in the darker corners where it wants to weld something hurtful with something human. I come from a long line of violence. In my poems I try to find a shape for the litany of terror to bring it into comprehension. The impossible. The terrible beauty of our lives: that we use them up, that the hunger fades. The impossible. Say it clearly and you make it beautiful, no matter what.

⌒⋙⋘⌒

Human Form
(Loyola Park)

Two weeks past Labor Day, the lifeguard towers pulled down,
replaced by Ukrainian crones on benches, chattering
beyond the Yuppie jogging suit, scoring crack from a second

jogging suit, which nods. Blink eyes and the deal's done,
the black guy ambling off, the doctor/lawyer/investment banker
unlocking the door of his BMW. Mexican Independence Day,

raised banderas snapping beside braziers, women
in armchair circles, men kicking soccer balls, careful
not to spill their cans of Pabst. Local color:

that's the way to start. Voice off, long shot of the lake.
Caption: *portrait of the author circa Nineteen
Ninety One (or two or three).* Time when the gods

descend to walk the evening, human form. May the author
now erase himself? He is tired of his small
mourning self. He has a working title: *Poem Without*

A Body Count. And yet. Did the gods descend to bring
his mother back in last night's dream, bald from the chemo,
raising herself from the car, one shoe off, that's all?

Close up to the author, long shot of the lake, empty beach
but for this couple, operatically obese,
each of them headphoned to a metal detector, cumbersome

back and forth along the sand, like stitchery.
The woman gestures and the man grunts back. (May the author
now erase himself?) The woman bends down. This shape

she's taken, now slowly it sifts through the sand with a trowel.
Catch anything? Bottlecaps, quarters, someone's
cheap wedding ring, electroplated, gleaming. Yet this

is not a wedding ring but a coal, glowing as the woman—
believe me as I say this—places it upon
the author's tongue. For do the gods not have the power

to bestow such gifts of vision? And does the coal not burn me
even now as I speak? I am nine again and helping her
to stack the canned goods and radio batteries

in the basement fallout shelter, for Khrushchev is sending
missiles to Cuba, and if my father comes home,
tomorrow or next week, the room will be prepared

and we shall enter it as if we were whole,
a family. The coal searing orange, my tongue
composed of fire. My happiness as I hand her soup cans,

bags of rice. And from the flame I watch her hand reach out
to touch my hair, run fingers through it absently.
Of fire she has fashioned me, of sparks

flaring out with her strokes, cascading, acetylene white.

The Form of "Human Form"

I HAVE A FRIEND WHOSE POETRY I DEARLY LOVE. AND YET, WHEN WE SIT DOWN TO TALK ABOUT writing, we argue. This is not surprising, for our styles are considerably different, our aesthetics are at odds with one another's, and we draw our inspiration from rather different influences. Over the years our disagreements have become something of a shtick, performances which other friends allow us to indulge in at parties, perhaps because they take pity on our need for such rituals. Yet the fact that we battle does not diminish my genuine respect for his writing and ideas, and from time to time I find that when I am writing poems I end up writing to my friend—or writing against something he has said, not so much to disagree with his notions as to test them, to see what happens when I try to put some of his theoretical propositions into action in my own work.

To gravely oversimplify matters, I could say that my friend Dean agrees with Marjorie Perloff's subversion of Creeley's famous dictum that "form is never more than an extension of content," which Perloff amends to read "form is never more than an extension of theory." Dean is fond of using terms drawn from deconstruction, from the theoretical essays of the Language Writers, and so forth. He by no means hews to a strict party line in his use of these terms, but when I hear him allude to the "exploded self," hear him claim that the speaker of the poem is merely or invariably an intellectual construct, hear him talk about his poetry's need to "demystify" our presuppositions about a poem's form and content, I end up feeling a mixture of agreement and distress. To place faith in the speaking voice that you have developed in poems over the years does not necessarily make you a horse returning to its stall during a barnfire. And there are some obsessive subjects that each of us possesses which, try as we might, we can't demystify.

To put it less obliquely, the poems that I care the most about deal with emotive basics. Yet one of life's most exasperating ironies is that emotive basics tend to remain wholly mysterious. "Human Form" began as an attempt to both describe a walk in my neighborhood in Chicago, and to talk back to my friend Dean about some of his ideas about poetry. But soon I realized that beneath these motives was a deeper issue: my mother has been dead for several years, and I still don't believe it. My walk and imaginary dialogue with Dean acted as a trigger for a long buried memory of my mother, one which suddenly emerged with all the intensity of a vision. I recalled my incredible sense of happiness during the Cuban missile crisis, when I helped my mother store food in the fallout shelter that we'd built in our basement. Somehow, the notion of my family, so distant from one another—and now, I see, so dysfunctional—huddling together in our basement to await some Civil Defense all clear, was a vision, however bizarre, of paradise. Like any ars poetica, "Human Form" is less a description of one's theory of poetry than it is a search for poetry's sources, which lie in astonishment and not in theory.

Charles Wright

Ars Poetica

I like it back here

Under the green swatch of the pepper tree and the aloe vera.
I like it because the wind strips down the leaves without a word.
I like it because the wind repeats itself,

                                    and the leaves do.

I like it because I'm better here than I am there,

Surrounded by fetishes and figures of speech:
Dog's tooth and whale's tooth, my father's shoe, the dead weight
Of winter, the inarticulation of joy. . .

The spirits are everywhere.

And once I have them called down from the sky, and spinning and
        dancing in the palm of my hand,
What will it satisfy?
                        I'll still have

The voices rising out of the ground,
The fallen star my blood feeds,

                        this business I waste my heart on.

And nothing stops that.

ONE OF THE 20 POEMS WRITTEN IN A SERIES, OVER A PERIOD OF TIME, AFTER HAVING HEARD A
John Cage concert, at the end of which, during the question and answer period, he
responded to one question with the answer, "I was giving myself instructions and carry-
ing them out." I thought this to be a particularly witty and serious answer, and spent the
next couple of years doing the same thing in a bunch of poems. Such instructions as a
poem with no verbs, a poem with no definite point of reference, a poem written at one
sitting with no revisions, a poem with a verb in every line. And so on. It seemed impor-
tant that an ars poetica be included in the group, and this is it.

I wrote the poem in Laguna Beach, California, where I used to live. The room I
worked in there, a tiny, windowless space cut out of the back of the garage, was decorated
with pinned-up postcards on all four walls and little fetishes and memorabilia on all the
flat surfaces: if I couldn't see out, I would see in. The longer I stayed in that room, the deep-
er my poems went back into the past, and deeper into what the past held out in its reliquary
hands for me to sip from. I was there for seven years and wrote two books: *The Southern
Cross* and *The Other Side of the River*. A pepper tree over-dangled the door and an aloe vera
plant grew into shade. The rest of the poem seems self-explanatory to me, given the title.
My instructions to myself were to write an ars poetica, and I tried to carry them out.

James Wright

Ars Poetica: Some Recent Criticism

1.

I loved my country,
When I was a little boy.
Agnes is my aunt,
And she doesn't even know
If I love anything
On this God's
Green little apple.

I have no idea why Uncle Sherman
Who is dead
Fell in with her.
He wasn't all that drunk.
He longed all life long
To open a package store,
And he never did anything,
But he fell in with Agnes.
She is no more to me
Than my mind is,
Which I bless. She was a homely woman
In the snow, alone.

Sherman sang bad,
But he could sing.
I too have fallen in
With a luminous woman.

There must be something.

The only bright thing
Agnes ever did
That I know of
Was to get hurt and angry.
When Sherman met my other uncle
Emerson Buchanan, who thinks he is not dead,

At the wedding of Agnes
Uncle Emerson smirked:
"What's the use buying a cow,
When you can get the milk free?"

She didn't weep.
She got mad.
Mad means something.
"You guys are makin' fun
Out of me."

2.

She stank.
Her house stank.
I went down to see Uncle Sherman
One evening.
I had a lonely furlough
Out of the army.
He must have been
One of the heroes
Of love, because he lay down
With my Aunt Agnes
Twice at least.
Listen, lay down there,
Even when she went crazy.
She wept two weeping daughters,
But she did not cry.
I think she was too lonely
To weep for herself.

3.

I gather my Aunt Agnes
Into my veins.
I could tell you,
If you have read this far,
That the nut house in Cambridge
Where Agnes is dying
Is no more Harvard
Than you could ever be.
And I want to gather you back to my Ohio.
You could understand Aunt Agnes,
Sick, her eyes blackened,
Her one love dead.

4.

Why do I care for her,
That slob,
So fat and stupid?
One afternoon,
At Aetnaville, Ohio,
A broken goat escaped
From a carnival,
One of the hooch dances
They used to hold

Down by my river.
Scrawny the goat panicked
Down Agnes's alley,
Which is my country,
If you haven't noticed,
America,
Which I loved when I was young.

5.

That goat ran down the alley,
And many boys giggled
While they tried to stone our fellow
Goat to death.
And my Aunt Agnes,
Who stank and lied,
Threw stones back at the boys
And gathered the goat,
Nuts as she was,
Into her sloppy arms.

6.

Reader,
We had a lovely language,
We would not listen.

I don't believe in your god.
I don't believe my Aunt Agnes is a saint.
I don't believe the little boys
Who stoned the poor
Son of a bitch goat
Are charming Tom Sawyers.

I don't believe in the goat either.

7.

When I was a boy
I loved my country.

Ense petit placidam
Sub libertate quietem.

Hell, I ain't got nothing.
Ah, you bastards,

How I hate you.

On James Wright's "Ars Poetica: Some Recent Criticism"

JAMES WRIGHT'S POEM "ARS POETICA: SOME RECENT CRITICISM" IS THE OPENING PIECE IN his book *Two Citizens*, originally published in 1973. This is the most difficult and probably the least liked of Wright's seven major volumes, and the poem is certainly of a piece with the book. The very title is confusing, even self-contradictory, which is why my question to Wright about the poem was phrased to be about the title. "Does your poem 'Ars Poetica: Some Recent Criticism' deal with literary criticism?" I asked him on behalf of *The Paris Review* in 1972. He answered:

No, this is a poem about my Aunt Agnes, who is a very suffering woman, and has been dying slowly for many years. I get so damned angry about the difference between literary criticism and real life in this country that I thought I would write an ars poetica of my own, which is about what is really going on in this country. [1]

Just before this exchange, I had asked Wright about *Two Citizens*, and he said it was about himself and his wife Annie, with respect to both in Europe and America. He indicated that he both loved and hated America at that time, which was late in the Vietnam era, when America was a deeply divided nation. Wright said that "Americans, who are good people and a kind of lost people, are suffering very badly." He added that "*Two Citizens* begins with a curse on America. There are some savage poems about Ohio, my home, in that book. . . ." The curse to which he refers is, of course, the opening poem in the book, "Ars Poetica: Some Recent Criticism."

So this poem is about Wright's Aunt Agnes, about what he thought was really going on in this country at that time, and a curse. What it is not, at least in the explanations offered by the poet, is a poem mostly about his own practice of the art of poetry—which is how we would identify most ars poeticas. Aunt Agnes is not a particularly attractive character, as presented in this poem. When the poet visited her and her husband, Uncle Sherman, "She stank. / Her house stank"; she was a "slob, / So fat and stupid." Since then, she has been institutionalized and is now dying in "the nut house in Cambridge" (Ohio), which "Is no more Harvard / Than you could ever be." (I shall return to that "you.")

Aunt Agnes, however, did have two moments in her life for which the poet venerates her. First, at her wedding, when Sherman's brother Emerson Buchanan "smirked: / 'What's the use buying a cow, / When you can get the milk free?'," Agnes "didn't weep, / She got mad. / Mad means something." She was proud, a woman of character. Second, when a "broken goat" escaped from a carnival in Aetnaville, fled down Agnes's alley, and was stoned with murderous intent by a group of boys, "Aunt Agnes, / Who stank and lied, / Threw stones back at the boys / And gathered the goat, / Nuts as she was, / Into her sloppy arms."

The poem has seven sections; this story is told in the fourth and fifth and commented on in the sixth: "I don't believe my Aunt Agnes is a saint. / I don't believe the little boys / Who stoned the poor / Son of a bitch goat / Are charming Tom Sawyers." The two statements interestingly go in opposite directions. When Wright denies canonization to Agnes, he seems to be undercutting the point of his story, in which she is the hero and the boys are the villains; but when he similarly denies Tom Sawyerhood (a kind of cute, American canonization: despite their minor sins, these are basically good boys), he is *affirming* the point of his story. In point of fact, Wright despises these boys for the casual way in which they would take the life of the goat, and for their own pleasure.

The boys thus represent what James Wright hated about America, and about Ohio: this kind of casual predatoriness is precisely the attitude that caused the United States so much trouble during its excursion into Vietnam. We see characters like these boys in many other James Wright poems; they are the "stupid harly-Charlies" in "All the Beautiful Are Blameless," for example, who get the girl drunk, take her "swimming naked on the lake," and cause her death by drowning; they are the hunters in "Redwings" who believe, hopefully, of the birds: "It turns out/ You can kill them. / It turns out / You can make the earth absolutely clean." And, if the subject of literary criticism appears at all in the poem, it would seem that these boys are close kin to the critics. This, to me, is the only way to explain Wright's use of the word "you" in the passage already quoted: "the nut house in Cambridge . . . / Is no more Harvard / Than you could ever be." This is a terrible accusation to make against the critics, all of whom secretly hope that someday they will be associated with Harvard, the best university in the land. The poem of course ends with Wright's specific curse against the "you" of his poem, against the authors of the criticism referred to in the title: "Hell, I ain't got nothing. / Ah, you bastards, // How I hate you." [2]

When he says, "I ain't got nothing," Wright is identifying with Agnes one final time. Of course he has been associating himself with her throughout the poem; perhaps the strongest link between the two is established in the second stanza of the poem's first section, where Wright says of Agnes: "She is no more to me /Than my mind is." By using irony, Wright means to intensify the connection he is expressing. And just as the boys represent more than themselves in the poem, so does Agnes. Wright indicates obliquely what else she is in the first three lines of the poem: "I loved my country, / When I was a little boy. /Agnes is my aunt. . . ." Just as the evil little boys are associated with the predatory spirit of America and with the critics, Aunt Agnes is associated with the spirit of an earlier America, an America worthy of the poet's love. The identification is solidified in the fourth section, where Wright refers to "Agnes's alley, / Which is my country, / If you haven't noticed, / America, / Which I loved when I was young."

Back then, says Wright at the beginning of the sixth section, "We had a lovely language, / We would not listen." Now that he has grown, and the country has gone bad, all Wright has left of America is his language, with which he can still write poems. The concluding section begins by drawing our attention rather forcefully, and again ironically, to the subject of language: "When I was a boy / I loved my country. // *Ense petit placidam / Sub libertate quietem.*" The irony, of course, is that Wright should have recourse to Latin at so crucial a point in a poem so deeply concerned with America. But Latin was the learned language of Wright's youth; it is the language he studied with greatest care in high school. And his teacher was another venerated older woman. Thus the passage both takes us back to earlier America and reminds us of the spirit of Agnes. The lines themselves are both a threat and a prayer: by means of the sword (they say) he seeks a peaceful quiet in freedom. The threat is in tune with Wright's tough-guy stance, with the anger of Agnes, and with the curse that ends the poem.

Now that I have taken the poem apart, I think I can conclude that there probably are ways in which it is an authentic ars poetica. First, it represents accurately Wright's late-middle style, the laconic, staccato, tough-guy style of some of the New Poems in *Collected Poems* and of all of the poems in *Two Citizens*. Second, its negative attitudes— toward the brutes and toward America—are utterly typical of Wright's writings, from beginning to end. Third, its positive attitudes—toward the earlier America and toward such suffering but admirable characters as Aunt Agnes—are also utterly typical of all of Wright's poems. I hope this is close to what he had in mind.

Endnote

1. THE INTERVIEW WAS CONDUCTED IN THE APRIL FOLLOWING THE DEATH BY SUICIDE OF John Berryman, who was in a way responsible for the fact that this interview took place. My primary teachers at the University of Minnesota were Berryman and James Wright. I interviewed Berryman for *The Paris Review* in October of 1970 and he died in January of 1972, shortly before the interview appeared in the magazine. When I learned that he had jumped to the railroad tracks beneath the Washington Avenue bridge, it suddenly seemed desperately important that I interview Wright immediately; I think I must have felt that everyone I cared about was going to die soon. So I drove from Middlebury, Vermont, where I was living, to New York City, where Jim and I spent two afternoons talking in his kitchen. The interview is most easily found in my book *The World's Hieroglyphic Beauty: Five American Poets*, and my quotations are, respectively, from pages 209 and 208.

2. WRIGHT'S ACTUAL, REAL-LIFE ATTITUDE TOWARD CRITICS WAS AT BEST AMBIVALENT. I KNOW that he admired some of the things I wrote about him, particularly the essay on *The Branch Will Not Break* published in the student magazine at the University of Minnesota in 1963. Jim still had copies of this at several places in his files at the time of his death. In 1971, after I had written my review of *Collected Poems* for *The New York Times Book Review*, but before it was published, he came to Middlebury to read his poems and I told him I had done the review but did not indicate my opinion of the book. His only reply was a kind of terrified stare. Early in 1972, before I interviewed him for *The Paris Review*, I published an essay in *The Minnesota Review* in which I first took apart the structure of *Shall We Gather at the River* and then put it back together, this time with all the poems in

their proper order. During the interview, I then asked him about the structure of the book. In his answer he begins by being polite to the critic, then answers him with scorn: "It was very carefully written to move in that way. Whether it came off or not is another question, and not for me to judge. . . . Like hell! I know damn well that that book is perfectly constructed, and I knew exactly what I was doing from the very first syllable to the very last one." Among the juvenile poems published in the Wright issue of *The Gettysburg Review* (Winter 1990) is one called "To Critics, and to Hell with Them"; the poem is typical of many that Wright wrote, but did not always publish, throughout his life.

by Peter Stitt

Poetry

We're in a new state, and the dandelions
are strange, thin-stemmed and somehow sophisticated-
looking, a kind of botanical west coast cool.
But I notice the bees still plunder them,
even on this windless Monday the blossoms bobbing
an undulant syncopation I can't quite ignore.
The babies are asleep, and the heat when I enter you
is some true thing I'm dreaming, not a memory at all,
but the body's one life, constant, expansive, simultaneous.

I can hear you putter in the kitchen, domestic these days,
and I admit, what I'm imagining now
requires your body, but not mine, my mind,
but not yours, the counter, the sink, the cloudy light
sliding from your shoulders and over your breasts,
across your belly, a drop of saliva or sweat,
silver bauble on a hair and right before my eyes.

This life's already so familiar, I can tell what pot
you hold by its ping against the cabinet door.
I can hear the refrigerator uncatch,
its yawn of light, its full and satisfied hum.
But for some reason the weather's
gone and changed. Now a great flock of crows
rides a thermal up out of the trees along the creek,
the bees have taken cover, and upstairs
the babies murmur and stir. Outside the dandelions sway
in unison, a decorous, chilly dance.

Listen, soldiers, I'd sell out the nation
to see my wife come in this room
with my skin on her mind. I'd pledge myself
to Jesus to see the light on her face
I might generate inside her. If she doesn't,
if I don't, it will have nothing to do with art,
or war, or the soul's blind abandon.
It will have nothing to do with the weather
or the crows, or the dandelions panting away
in the wind, having started all this unawares,
ubiquitous for the bees and their droning yeoman imperatives:
the seasons, the sun, this great, odd, and unfathomable drive
toward the dark.

THE TITLE CAME LAST—"POETRY"—AND I FELT A LITTLE SILLY CALLING THE POEM THAT, BUT everything else I considered just seemed coy, at best, sometimes even dishonest. I wrote the poem on October 1, 1990, during the height of the military buildup preceding the Gulf War. At the time, writing a poem full of dandelions and sweet imaginary sex in the kitchen felt wrong, somehow. Trivial, escapist, self-centered. The trick, if I can call it that, is trusting the poem to find its own way. Maintain the language—the music and the cadence—and let the poem go. That may explain the odd leap in the final stanza, the apostrophic shift from lover to soldiers. The poem doesn't mean to explain itself or the art, so much as it means to enact it. Poetry—like any form of love and yearning—can exist in spite of the horror. Or maybe because of it.

Seven Days: An Ars Poetica

The stillborn calf lies near the fence where its mother licked the damp body, then left it. All afternoon she has stood beside a large, white rock in the middle of the pasture. She nuzzles it with her heavy neck and will not be lured away. This must be her purest intelligence, to accept what she expected, something sure, intractable, the whole focus of the afternoon's pale light.

* * *

I'm reading the stars to figure my place here below. I watch the constellations slide and spill across the sky. There are star charts geared and matched to our lives, but here is the real map we are born to and fixed on. Not even the night is still. We are spinning with the stars, and heaven must wheel as well.

* * *

Two girls were struck by lightening at the harbor mouth. An orange flame lifted them up and laid them down again. Their thin suits had been melted away. It's a miracle they survived. It's a miracle they were ever born at all.

* * *

Our son was born under a full moon. That night I walked through the orchard, and the orchard was changed as I was. There were blossoms on the fruit trees, more white blossoms on the dogwood, and the tiny clenched fists of bracken shimmered silver. My shadow fell beside the shadow of the trees like a luster on the grass, and wherever I looked there was light.

* * *

The sun is a star; what we see, we see by starlight: the clouds, the trees, the cliffs and harsh water. This light is heavenly; it has come to us a long way. It is resting now on a boy's pale arm, and his small hand that reaches for my shirt.

* * *

The world is made of names; my son is learning to speak. He has faith. He believes in things. Rock, I tell him, leaf. No, *this*, he says, holding the rock. *This*, he says, holding up the leaf.

* * *

I put asters in a small blue vase. Each morning they open, and they close again each night. Even in this dark room they follow a light which does not reach them. They have bodies. That is all the faith they need.

SEVERAL YEARS AGO I PUBLISHED *THE GEOGRAPHY OF HOME*, AN ARTIST'S BOOK CONSISTing of forty relief prints and a text running in a single, continuous line across its ninety-two pages. This text, oriented horizontally rather than vertically through the book, challenged certain fundamental assumptions about poems as I had learned to want to write them. It proved to be the stylistic and thematic germ for my subsequent book, *Days*, and my current work-in-progress, *Braver Deeds*.

There is an implicit hierarchy in the structural methodology of verse written in customary stanza and line. As the reader is led from the top of a poem to the bottom, lines are end-stopped or enjambed to provoke a deliberate emotional response, a response that is, by its nature, artificial. This strategy of stanza and line is perhaps no more artificial than any other at the poet's disposal, but at the very least the *democracy* of speech is forfeited. *Days* is an attempt to write poems of meaningful utterance that move from beginning to end horizontally. Their measure is emotive rather than syllabic or metrical. On the page they appear as brief, untitled prose pieces, but in conception and execution they are long, one line poems; the architectonics of stanza and line have been replaced by syntax, grammar, and rhythm. My aim is to write poems that one might figuratively walk along, rather than fall through. My intention is to quiet these poems, not to silence, but to equilibrium where a calm voice need not interrupt itself with self-consciousness or artifice but speak simply in the knowledge that the breath propelled represents a faithful utterance of the heart.

Drama is not the analog for being but merely its gesture; all events are correspondent in a horizontal hierarchy of significance. Too often in my earlier books I felt the seduction of the line had distorted the true subject of a poem, and misrepresented the real nature of my task as a writer. My chief preoccupations—the domestic, the mundane, and the seemingly superficial—lose what power and substance they do possess when they try to be more than they are. The line is a tool of this inflation.

I have found it more difficult to lie in prose, either through omission or amplification. Poems written in prose encourage—at least in me—a stricter honesty, and as a result the mysteries revealed—at least for now—seem more genuine and profound. I want to write with as much clarity as I can about those moments that hold only the essence of drama, those brief, disquieting moments that define our lives. Where the impulse might be to reflect and elaborate, to draw a broader reality from the moment at hand, I have tried in these new poems to pare away peripheral reflection to touch surely the moment, and to freeze it. The concept of a lyric moment is itself a conceit, of course; even the shortest poem takes time to read. But each instant understood thoroughly—understood as God might understand it—is of a caliber with any other, not because it has been demoted to some lowest common denominator, but because each is a kernel and a mirror of eternity.

Acknowledgments and Copyright Notices

About the Editors

Christopher Buckley is the author of many collections of poetry, including *With Dust, Leaves, Blue Autumn,* and *Dark Matter*. Editor of *On the Poetry of Philip Levine: Stranger to Nothing,* he teaches creative writing at West Chester State College in Pennsylvania.

Christopher Merrill's most recent books are *Watch Fire* (poetry), *The Grass of Another Country: A Journey Through the World of Soccer* (non-fiction), and *The Old Bridge: The Third Balkin War and the Age of the Refugee* (non-fiction). He edits the Peregrine Smith Poetry Series.